JOB, INC.

JOB, INC.

How To Turn Your Job Into Pay
Raises, Promotions, And Recognition

Carlos Roche

INSIDE FOLIO
BOOKS

Interior design by Sarah E. Holroyd
(http://sleepingcatbooks.com)
Cover design by Carlos Roche

ISBN-13: 978-1-5076-7619-6

To my wife and children (Mari, Kai, and Carlitos), I loved you, I love you, and I will always love you.

When all the logical consequences of an innovation are presented simultaneously, the shock to habits is so great that men tend to reject the whole, whereas, if they had been invited to take one step every ten or twenty years, they could have been coaxed along the path of progress without much resistance.

～Bertrand Russell

Table of Contents

Preface. xi
Introduction. xiii
  What is an Employeepreneur?. xiv
  Making Even More Money than Your Boss. xv
  A Lobster. xvi
Chapter 1
The Magic of Self-Esteem—The #1 Step to Raising Your
Own Paycheck. 1
Chapter 2
Frankenstein. 8
Chapter 3
The Industrial Revolution and Your Limited Salary. . . . 14
Chapter 4
The Age of Enlightenment & Your Unlimited Income . . 21
Chapter 5
From Employee to Employeepreneur. 28
  What Does It Take?. 28
  Making the Move. 31
  Additional Concepts to Keep in Mind. 38
Chapter 6
Case Study: Discover How I Raised My Own
Salary At My Job By 84%. I Used 4 Skills You
Use Every Day!. 47
Chapter 7
Creating Your Influential Team. 65
  The Team. 65
  Finding Experts. 67
  Mentors and coaches 70
Chapter 8
Personal Resources to Boost Your Salary. 74
  Your personal resources. 75

Chapter 9
Raising Your Salary As Often As You Want 84
Chapter 10
The Function of a Business. 91
   The function of money 94
   What you sell 96
Chapter 11
Presenting Your Ideas 98
   The problem 99
   The solution 99
   The competition 100
   Marketing and sales 100
   Your execution 101
   A note about design. 101
Chapter 12
Your Personal Brand Means Money 103
Chapter 13
The New Consumer 107
   Bargain hunter vs. value hunter. 108
   Wait for solutions vs. find their own 109
   Trust advertising vs. distrust advertising 110
   Trust product information vs. read product
   information. 111
   Few options vs. too many options 111
   Disconnected vs. connected 112
Chapter 14
Creating Products and Services. 114
   Identify the problem 118
   Gather information 120
   Filter the information. 122
   Develop your product or service 123
Chapter 15
Marketing for Employeepreneurs 125
   The message. 126
   The audience. 133
   The media 137

Chapter 16

Direct Marketing. 138

    Email Marketing 138

    Direct mail marketing (sales letters). 140

    Networking and social media 150

Chapter 17

Customers and Lead Generation. 156

    Getting leads. 161

    Managing leads 162

    Converting leads 163

Chapter 18

Legal Issues and Negotiations 165

    Compensation 166

    Residual income. 167

    Survival beneficiary 167

    New products, services, and innovations. 168

Chapter 19

Gratitude. 170

Chapter 20

Goal Setting. 173

Chapter 21

Creating Your Desired Lifestyle. 176

Afterword 180

The question isn't who is going to let me; it's who is going to stop me.
〜Ayn Rand

Preface

I wrote this book with only one intention in mind: *to show employees from all over the world how they can create the lifestyle they dream of at their present jobs.*

This book is not intended to advance your career (even though it will). It is intended to help you make more money than your immediate boss or manager—a lot more money. You will not find the usual talk about becoming more of a company man or woman. You will not read about working harder, longer hours or about earning your employer's favor.

You will hear none of that because this book is for you and about you, not about your employer. It is not about becoming a better employee or arriving on time, it is about reclaiming the time and riches that the industrial revolution and current global labor system stole from you.

As an employee and as a person you have needs, wants, and desires that the current employer–employee arrangement can't satisfy on a personal or financial level. For many of us, the joy, benefits, and meaning of work have been reduced to a meaningless chore we do to get limited amounts of money in order to save a little (in banks where it loses value and is unprotected), eat, and pay our bills.

When we think about work the first thing that comes to mind is any activity we do on behalf of someone else to make money. But this definition of work has been created by the global labor system that intends to perpetuate the status quo.

Work is a natural expression of who we are. The dictionary definition of it is wrong. This definition is in agreement with the status quo.

We can't be personally fulfilled unless we do meaningful work (self-expression), or at least well-remunerated work. But as we will see, well-remunerated is not in accord with companies' policies. As an employee, you can make more money than you are making right now, but for that to happen you must decide to change gears and start using your intellect, your expertise and your employer's resources in a different way. Don't wait for a raise that may never come, raise it yourself.

Introduction

Have you ever wondered, Why are we employees? Why are we forced to wake up early in the morning and spend eight or ten hours stuck in an office or other location doing things that we might love but most likely we hate?

The easy answer is that we have to pay our bills. We want to buy things, and we need money. Employers give us money, we give them our time and skills (current and future). To work—for someone else—is the only life we have ever known in order to make money. It is what our parents did, and it's what most of us do.

We are creatures of habit. Most of the time, we follow in the footsteps of the people we love and respect. But our parents, and their parents, and likely generations of their parents before them, learned to be employees because of the well-crafted plan of the creators of the Industrial Revolution to monopolize and lay claim to the global workforce. They needed cheap and easily replaceable labor or employees.

However, the word employee is not synonymous with the word low wages or salary stagnation. Every business regardless of its size has many resources. Any employee with the right ideas can put these assets to work and make money for the company and for himself. No company on earth can take full advantage of all its resources. The *Employeepreneur* concept is simple. However, it is sure to meet skepticism, prejudice, fear, and politics throughout the business world because the conventional mentality is that you—the employee—shouldn't make a lot of money. This is the current mindset in any industry, company or governmental institution all over the world.

Have no doubt—this book is about you and how you can make more money at your job. It's about effectively monetizing the value and expertise you possess right now in your current position. It's about empowering you to raise your salary and live the life you want.

I hope this book can help you start to live that life. Certainly, it can help you earn more money—using that money to fulfill your fantasies is completely up to you.

WHAT IS AN EMPLOYEEPRENEUR?

An employeepreneur is someone who has found a way to effectively use his employer's connections, equipment, staff, and other resources to raise his own salary as often as he wants and create his own schedule—working the hours, days, and weeks he chooses—in order to live the life he has always dreamed of. This applies to a salaried employee or a commission-based salary worker or agent.

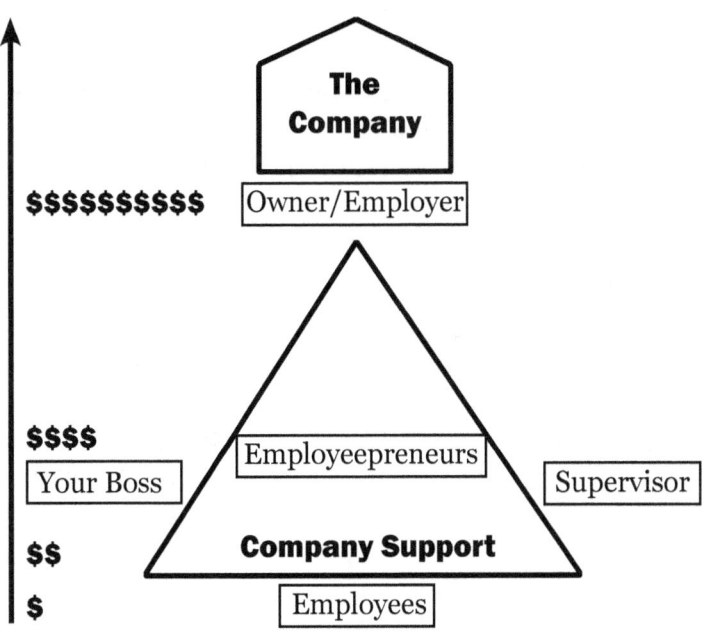

MAKING EVEN MORE MONEY THAN YOUR BOSS

Whoever your boss is, and whatever his role, just like you, he works for the company. Even if he owns the company, he is still working to make it successful. His job and your job in many ways are exactly the same. Don't let the hierarchical structure and corporate ladder concept make you believe that you have to earn less than anyone in the company. Everyone's goal is to grow the company financially. Moreover, in today's world, the opportunities that you have to make a difference in your company—no matter your role!—can be tremendous.

Everyone can help increase a company's revenue, whether by bringing in a new customer, improving an existing product or service, or creating a new product or service.

If you find ways to impact the company's bottom line, your boss will become your champion. He or she will be happy to work on the projects you create and for the customers you bring to the business—because you will be making the company money.

If you follow the strategies laid out in this book, your boss or employer will gladly serve your customers, manage your projects, and collect payments that you will have the opportunity to share. For hundreds of years, workers like you have felt limited in their potential to create riches for their employers and for themselves. It is time to unlock that hidden potential and dramatically increase your salary.

If you have any questions, or would like to share your own experiences applying the information in this book, please tell us about it through email at carlos@thejobpreneur.com.

A LOBSTER

A lobster, when removed from the water and placed on the rocks, does not have enough survival sense to work her way back into the sea. She will wait patiently for the sea to come and get her and to return her safely back into the water.

If the sea doesn't come, she will remain where she is and she will die—although even the slightest effort would have enabled her to reach the waves just a few yards away and save her life.

This world is full of "people-lobsters"—millions of people stranded on the rocks of indecision and procrastination. Instead of putting forth their own energies, they wait for some grand wave of fortune to come and suddenly give them riches.

What type of person are you?

This book is not for lobsters...

Chapter 1
The Magic of Self-Esteem—
The #1 Step to Raising
Your Own Paycheck

*Tell me how a person judges his or her self-esteem,
and I will tell you how that person operates at work,
in love, in sex, in parenting, in every important
aspect of existence—and how high he or she is likely
to rise. The reputation you have with yourself—your
self-esteem—is the single most important factor for a
fulfilling life.*
   ⌒Dr. Nathaniel Branden

Most people (including myself until recently) have
no idea what self-esteem really is and how it affects us
on a daily basis. No one tells us much about it, and what
little we are told about it is mostly inaccurate because
the information in the mainstream media and general
society is flat-out wrong. Self-esteem can be an ally
or an enemy. When self-esteem becomes an enemy,
it can be a lethal and uncontrollable one because it's
similar to having an enemy living inside of you.
   Millions of people go through life without really
understanding how low self-esteem affects every area
of their life and destroys self-respect, self-dignity, and
integrity. The consequences of low self-esteem can be
so devastating to a person's life that most of the personal failures in careers, parenting, or marriages find
their roots in low self-esteem.

You can see the greatest low self-esteem phenom-enon at the end of every year as people declare their New Year's resolutions. They want to accomplish so many things, but the minute the fuzzy, good New Year feeling wears off, so do their dreams. The truth is that most people don't believe that they deserve to have what they desire.

Our educational system not only teaches us to make a living, to live paycheck by paycheck, it also builds a sense of identity by stuffing our minds full of irrel-evant information. Building positive self-esteem is nowhere to be found in the factory-style school system that builds our characters and social entities.

The system prepares us to make a living as employ-ees, and sets us up to fail miserably when it comes to understanding ourselves and discovering the amazing forces that hide within us.

I spent years trying to figure out why there was a wall around me, blocking me from achieving the goals and objectives I'd set for myself. Why, even if I wanted financial freedom, deep down I felt and acted as if I didn't deserve it. Why I constantly sabotaged myself and didn't see most of my projects through.

I felt like I was running on a hamster wheel. Repeat-edly I would end up in the same place, with the same circumstances and the same frustration, and I just couldn't understand why. I would cry when no one could see me. In frustration I would secretly think about suicide.

I arrived at the conclusion that I was genetically defective. There was something wrong with me I needed to fix. I needed to correct myself but I didn't know how. I just knew that I didn't want to continue to live like that.

My desire to succeed and to give my family what I dreamed was so great that it made every failure even more painful. But you see, I was creating that failure. I was acting from a place of very low self-esteem. I am sure that I was not alone. There are many people who have no idea what or who is stopping them. People who bump against the same mistakes time and time again and don't know why.

Self-esteem, without a doubt, will be the most important factor in your pursuit to increase your own paycheck. The more you believe and think you deserve, the more you will have and get. In Western society, we tend to link our personal value to the amount of money we make. Money is a very strong driver of social status. But it is an external motivator. Having positive self-esteem will motivate you from the inside out.

When I discovered the work of Dr. Nathaniel Branden and started using his material, my life took a turn for the unknown. Something was ignited within me and my life perspective changed completely. I suddenly understood that I could accomplish everything my heart desires.

Do yourself a favor: run to Amazon and get a copy of Dr. Nathaniel Branden's *The Six Pillars of Self-Esteem*. It is, in my opinion, the best book written on the subject. In it, he talks about some simple exercises that transformed my life. These exercises are so simple that you might disregard them as something trivial.

While practicing these exercises, I felt that something powerful stormed into my unconscious mind and started to reveal the true me to myself. It was very transformative and I am sure the process will have the same effect on you.

Before you can raise your own paycheck, you need to believe that you deserve that money, that promotion, and that recognition. This is so true because if the change doesn't happen inside first, it's nearly impossible for it to happen outside. And if it does manage to happen outside, most likely it won't last.

Many people believe that just because we are children of God, we should have high self-esteem. Unfortunately, it's not that easy. Nothing is free. There's always some work involved, and the work to improve self-esteem should happen in the minds and hearts of every person on the planet.

The exercise (adapted from Dr. Branden's work) consists of reading the sentence stems and questions below, and completing or answering as fast as possible, giving 5 endings to each sentence or answer. Do this exercise in the morning when you wake up and at night before you go to bed. It should take about 10 minutes each time.

Here are the sentence stems and questions:

If I am more accepting of my thoughts and ideas...
1.
2.
3.
4.
5.

If I am more accepting of my body...
1.
2.
3.
4.
5.

If I am more accepting of my fears...
1.
2.
3.
4.
5.

If I am more accepting of my excitement...
1.
2.
3.
4.
5.

If I bring 5% more awareness to my relationships with my family, wife, friends, and kids, what would happen?
1.
2.
3.
4.
5.

If I bring 5% more awareness to my relationships with my boss and co-workers, what would happen?

1.

2.

3.

4.

5.

If I bring 5% more awareness to the evolution of my job mindset, what would happen?

1.

2.

3.

4.

5.

If I were confident that I would cope, succeed, and thrive in every challenge and opportunity I face in my future, what would happen?

1.

2.

3.

4.

5.

If I bring 5% more awareness to how I make money at my job, what would happen?

1.

2.

3.

4.

5.

If it were possible for me to raise my paycheck right now, what would I do with the money?

1.

2.

3.

4.

5.

You can modify the questions to adapt them to any situation or circumstance you feel that you want to improve in your life.

As you do this exercise of self-discovery to increase your self-esteem, you will begin to feel a sense of power. Something you may have never experienced before, something personal and unique. This new realization that you righteously deserve happiness, love, health, and money will catapult you far in your new path to raising your own paycheck at work, and the information you'll discover in the following pages will also be of great help.

Go ahead, try it. Start raising your paycheck from the inside.

Chapter 2
Frankenstein

Technologically we now have [six billion billionaires] on Spaceship Earth who are entirely unaware of their good fortune. Unbeknownst to [us our] legacy is being held in probate by general ignorance, fear, selfishness, and a myriad of paralyzing professional, licensing, zoning, building laws and the like, as bureaucratically maintained by the incumbent power structures.
　　　　　　∼R. Buckminster Fuller, Critical Path

We all know about Frankenstein's monster, the creature created by Victor Frankenstein, the scientist in the novel by Mary Shelley. It's the classic that gave birth to science fiction and popularized horror stories all over the world. But Mary Shelley didn't just write a horror story; she gave life, a voice, and actions to one of humanity's toughest problems: the creation of systems that turn around and kill us, or at least make us terribly unhappy.

Since we created the first settled societies, we have been creatingsocial systems to make life easier and to progress. And we have moved forward far beyond the conditions our forefathers used to live in. I have no doubt in my mind about it, because today we live more comfortable lives. But we have not moved as a people, as a global community of people, who have enough resources to create heaven on earth—if not on a personal level, at least on a financial level.

Many elements of the governmental, religious, educational, and family unit systems we put in place hold us back as a whole, hinder progress, and sometimes even keep us years, if not centuries, in ignorance. As you already know, the dictionary defines a system as "a set of connected things or parts [and I add: people] forming a complex whole." When a system takes cultural hold of a society, the mass social mindset stops questioning its drawbacks and subjects itself to the new social or belief system.

Many of the discoveries and inventions we have made over the last 200 years could have been made thousands of years ago. The earth elements that the Wright brothers used to take flight have been present on the planet for thousands of years. Orville Wright wrote to a friend, "Isn't it astonishing that all these secrets have been preserved for so many years just so we could discover them!" But these have never been "secrets." Newton and many other scientists before and after him introduced us to a whole new world of technological possibilities and advances in society. Their discoveries gave birth to the industrial revolution and the modern world in which we live today.

The number one problem with systems is that we tend to accept them as a matter of fact and don't question them. For many years the authority of the land in Europe, the Catholic Church, said that the earth was flat, and this was accepted by nearly all. People were even burned alive for just saying that it was round or any other shape they imagined.

In present-day India there are social caste systems that inflict inferiority on the minds, hearts, and social expression of groups of people. According to the *Gale Encyclopedia of U.S. History*, by the eighteenth century indentured servants (white slaves) outnumbered African slaves in the North American British colonies. As victims and oppressors, we get comfortable, we get complacent, and we adapt to the new situation of indentured servitude, slavery, or financial bondage, as we can see in the current global labor system.

The Sumerians created the first agricultural system known to man and today we use it to wage war on competitive markets and to create systematic lack of food and hunger in the world. The Prussians created the first military schools to discipline and build loyal soldiers for their army. They created the most organized army of its time due to their ordered and disciplined military schooling system. Modern societies adapted this military school model to feed the global labor system initiated by the industrial revolution.

As an employee, you are expected to limit your intellectual capabilities to executing your job description or performing the job you are paid to do and nothing else. The systematic belief or habit is: *go to work, do your job, and go home to rest to come to work again.* But this belief in the global labor system is not sustainable. People will soon start to realize that their job description is not the only thing they can do at their workplace. They will start to look at their jobs as a platform for the creation of riches—not only for their employers, but also for themselves—and this is adding to this new trend.

In Mary Shelley's book, the monster killed his creator because artificial systems usually kill real life. Take the economy concept we have created. It's a concept based on lack and the management of scarce resources, even though we have more resources than we can consume on the planet and the means to create new ones. But this economic system creates vast amounts of money for some and leaves the rest without even the most basic necessities.

The systems we put in place suffocate the life and joy of those they are supposed to serve and protect. Millions of suffering people from all over the world are subject to systems that oppress and inhibit their personal and financial development. They experience the absurdities we have built into these systems in our societies.

Take the example of a young Serbian immigrant who came to America to realize his dream of building the first power station in the Niagara Falls, using alternating current, a new concept at the time, to power New York.

Nikola Tesla would have fit right in if he had come to be part of the norm, using the existent electrical system. But he didn't fit because he had strange ideas, like the creation of an alternating current (AC) motor.

The man who gave us the modern world of electricity, radio, internet, remote control, electric cars, sophisticated weapons, and even wireless electricity had to dig holes for a year in New York to make a living before he had the opportunity to realize his vision.

Even though the elite groups of the time knew exactly the benefits Tesla's success could bring to humanity. Tesla also had to face the systematic monster of the time.

Another notable example of the time was the air brake for trains invented by George Westinghouse. He had to wait more than 20 years for the US Congress to legislate a mandate for trains to be able to use his new invention. Prior to the invention of the air brake, it was very difficult for trains to stop quickly. The conductor had to reverse the steam flow to use the engine as the brakes. But Congress didn't see the need for the new technology, or lobbying interests of the time prevented its introduction. Borrowing from Mary Shelley's book, the monster had killed its creator.

What does all this have to do with your salary? Your weekly, bi-weekly, or monthly pay check is not an isolated event. It is part of a systematic process that keeps millions of people in financial bondage. To free your salary from the limitations of the hours you work and that your job description imposes on it, you will need to engage your mind in a different way. You will need to start looking at your employer's overall operations as your own to make money with.

So your challenge as an employeepreneur is not only a matter of increasing your salary, it's also a matter of demystifying old labor systems'myths and breaking old habits related to what you do for money.As an employeepreneur, you will be challenging the cultural mindset of "this is how we have done it for hundreds of years, no need to change it." You will be facing the same systemic Frankenstein's monsters that Newton,

Westinghouse, Tesla, and many others faced in their time to create the world they imagined for themselves and the rest of humanity. You will face this monster in yourself, in your family and friends, and in society in general. But you need to also understand that you are the first and most important person you need to work on. You must "unboss" first your mind and then your actions. As entrepreneur and motivational speaker Jim Rohn said, "Work harder on yourself than you do on your job." Open your eyes and understand that systems like the global labor scheme can get the best of you only if you allow it. Your mind is the last frontier. I recently watched one of the Harry Potter movies with my kids and they are fascinated by the effects and magical world in the movies. I often tell them that they also live in a magical world and that their minds are their magic wands. Your mind is your most powerful weapon in confronting and conquering the job system we live in today.

The labor system is set up to make you trade time for money. When you become an employeepreneur, you trade ideas for money, and you have a fertile ground right at your workplace to do it. You can get out of the hamster wheel and start taking advantage of your employer's resources.

As a former forex trader, one of the most important lessons I learned was "when you see the masses going in one direction, go the opposite way."

Chapter 3
The Industrial
Revolution and Your
Limited Salary

The Industrial Revolution was a period in human history (1700–1900) when people began to create groundbreaking and efficient new methods of manufacturing as well as engineering new modes of transportation to deliver those manufactured goods to customers. Unlike many other revolutions, this one was not started by the masses. Instead, it was started in England—spreading to continental Europe and then to the United States—by a very limited and wealthy group of investors who pooled money together to fund the emerging industries of the time (industrial farming, transportation, oil production, energy, technology, banking, finance, electricity, and industrial manufacturing).

These new commercial enterprises needed people—employees—to fuel their growth, because, as you already know, without *you* a company is nothing more than a building full of material and machinery. Without *you*, a company is dead. But first they had to mold people like you (and me) into more malleable human beings, able to buy in to a vision of the world that put the corporation above the individual. They had to make people like you believe that a good salary should be everyone's highest aspiration. They had to teach people like you to be happy with a salaried job, and a limited life. The school system became the perfect platform to inculcate these beliefs and create well-behaved employees. We have been trained well to accept the status quo and see the working world as something we can do nothing about. But why should this be true? Who says we have to work until our bodies can't take it anymore? Who says we have to live our lives according to someone else's script? Who says we can't retire from our jobs and leave our bosses there— working for us?

We were trained to get up early in the morning and go to school in order to learn about general subjects that have nothing to do with our particular interests and talents, but everything to do with training our minds to fall in line and not rock the boat. As children, we spend seven to eight hours in a closed room so that we don't later feel claustrophobic in our factories or offices, with perhaps only a short break for lunch as the only respite of the day. The subjects taught in school, and the testing methods we are subjected to, are designed to stunt our thinking ability and make us less inclined to question things. Everything you need to succeed in school is provided to you. You have no reason to look elsewhere.

This system of education was the perfect way to create employees that would let the Industrial Revolution continue, and create riches only for those who were already wealthy.

Of course I know the importance of a good education, but education does not mean training young minds to obey archaic rules and become silent pawns in oppressive labor systems. When we as children are

grouped together to learn about subjects of no personal interest to us, we are merely being trained to be
part of a workforce that will deprive us of our time
and our potential riches.

During the Industrial Revolution, children had to
work the same hours and engage in the same brutal
forms of labor as adults, but as we became more civi-
lized and socialized, we couldn't continue doing that
to our kids. Our educational system served as a different, more humane method to get children into the
system as early as possible. You need to understand
that the industrial system has been designed to sus-
tain itself. And it has dug itself so deeply into our society that it has become almost invisible.

The scheme I am talking about hides behind the
idea of getting good grades in school to change the way
we think. We have built a global social code insisting
on grades and formal education being so important
that some people even commit suicide when they
don't pass a test or can't graduate from college. But
the whole educational system—from kindergarten
to university—is merely preparation for working for
someone else, in a job with a very specific and limited
description and very specific and limited salary.

As an employee, your salary has a history attached
to it. It is a history that started at the dawn of the
Industrial Revolution. It developed over many
decades of labor abuse, strikes, complaints, the creation of unions, government intervention, and many
other factors. You already know that companies don't
have your best interests at heart. What you may not
know is that they intentionally keep you constrained

financially so that you have no choice but to come back to work tomorrow, next week, next month, and next year. But these constraints are merely illusions—they can block you only if you believe in them. Today, there's a whole segment in business dedicated to researching salaries, comparing them, informing people, and training you how to fight for what you ought to be paid according to your profession and experience. You think this is helping you, but it is really only designed to maintain the status quo. It only reinforces the powerful belief that employees should be paid a limited and fixed amount of money, tied to experience and not to results. But why? Shouldn't we be compensated based on our production and intellectual contribution, and how much we can innovate to deliver increased profits? Shouldn't we be properly incentivized to help our employer's business grow? Capping salaries at a fixed number hurts the employer as well as the employee. But we have come to accept this salary limitation practice (which goes against human nature) in part because we are prepared for it from an early age in our school system. This is the result of many years of priming our subconscious minds in our educational system to accept these and many other practices. Priming is the act of making something ready; it is the act of influencing people's behavior using perception, words, and the environment or surroundings. But the most direct relation we can find in our school system to our limited salaries is the report card. It doesn't matter how smart, brilliant, or talented you are, you will never go above 100%. Our grading system is the perfect predecessor of our limited salaries.

Employers all over the world follow what is called in the business world "best practices." These are standard ways of operating that you find in all industries across the commercial and business world. Most of these practices are centuries old, but no one questions them because how can you question the best? But they are only the best practices because someone on the corporate side decided that they are. So everyone accepts the status quo: "This is my salary, only my boss or employer can raise it, and so I have to wait for them to do it."

We tell ourselves stories to keep us going: "If they don't give me a raise by this date, I will ask. And if they still don't give me a raise, I will work harder and stay longer hours without asking them to pay me overtime. Maybe then I will prove I deserve it." We allow our employer to exert tremendous power over our personal and financial lives when we think this way. We give them all of the control. And the reason that this seems completely normal to us is because of the indoctrination we receive in schools at an early age. We see the school as a father figure—the authority that we must obey and respect. When we finish school and join adult society, in our minds we replace school with other institutions: corporations, churches, hospitals, doctors, police officers, government officials, etc.

This game of authority and hierarchical structure has a direct impact on how much money we think we should earn. But it has nothing to do with our value as a person or as a professional. The game is in place to maintain the status quo. If you play it, you can't win. I can't pretend to tell you that I can change the game myself, but at least I can explain how it works. R. Buckminster Fuller said it best: "You never change things by fighting the existing reality. To change something, build a new model that makes the existing model obsolete."

The Industrial Revolution was about buying your time and your manual labor for pennies on the dollar, and many companies continue to follow this mode of thought. This is the business model on which the revolution was developed. This model maintains the belief that you should be happy merely to have a job and pay your bills.

But this model can't continue to function in a global economy where every individual should be trying to develop his or her intellectual capabilities to grow personally and financially.

There is a new model emerging from the old one, and this new model is conceptual. People are realizing the tremendous power that they possess within themselves to create anything they want. They are looking for alternative ways to live their lives. This is a new world of ideas, imagination, and innovation. The business world as we know it today will not exist in ten or twenty years. The business world as we know it has entered a period of profound change—a second Industrial Revolution that is shaping new ways of doing business all over the world. Some people try to increase their salaries by looking for a part-time job or even a second full-time job. But others—like you— are realizing that the best place to raise their salaries is where they are now, at their present job. Your salary belongs to you. It is in your control—and no institution, person, or company can keep your income in check if you apply your intellect to raise it as high as you want to.

Now that you have a better understanding of what brought you to this point in your professional life, I can show you how to go from having a fixed salary as an employee to building an unlimited income as an employeepreneur—without quitting your job or looking for another one.

Chapter 4
The Age of Enlightenment & Your Unlimited Income

The real source of wealth and capital in this new era is not material things. It is the human mind, the human spirit, the human imagination, and our faith in the future.
~ Steve Forbes

According to Wikipedia, "the Age of Enlightenment (or simply the Enlightenment or Age of Reason) was a cultural movement of intellectuals in 18th century Europe and the American colonies. Its purpose was to reform society using reason (rather than tradition, faith and revelation) and advance knowledge through science."

During the Enlightenment, Baruch Spinoza, Newton, Voltaire, and many others taught that people should not believe anything that authorities (churches, kings, governments, etc.) tell them. They taught people to test ideas for themselves and come to their own conclusions.

This kind of thinking was revolutionary at a time when the church and the state dictated what people ought to believe and how they must behave. The Enlightenment was a time of increased interest in learning about science, logic, and reason. Traditional beliefs, dogmas, and faith-based ways of living were re-examined and sometimes rejected completely.

Today, all across the world, a second Age of Enlightenment is taking place. People from all walks of life are waking up to the realization that we have been tricked into believing in a system that deprives us of our three most precious gifts: time, liberty of movement, and wealth.

As employees we sell our time and expertise for little money—and most employers want to keep it that way, because it is supremely convenient and enriching for them. You will go to work next week because you didn't make enough money last week. It's an endless cycle. We need to make money to deal with our financial obligations. But selling our skills, time, future expertise, and knowledge for the same fixed salary, week after week, doesn't make sense. It doesn't truly help the employer and it certainly doesn't help you, or let you ever escape the system.

We are living in an age of change far superior to what started in Europe in the second half of the 18th century. Everything that we believed would last forever is crumbling. Banking systems are collapsing. Commercial institutions are falling apart. Access to wealth is becoming more and more open—we can all be employeepreneurs in our employer's business, and we can all reach a world of potential customers in today's interconnected world.

Your job, whatever it may be, is no exception. Every industry, big or small, is changing. If you are doing the same thing you did a year ago, your boss is behind the curve. He or she is surely trying to find a way to automate whatever it is you do— to do it with less expense or add more duties to your job description.

You need to increase your value every day. Today, just like during the Enlightenment period, everyone has access to the same information. Many people say that information is power, but, in reality, it is merely potential power. It all depends on what you do with it. The information itself isn't valuable alone. Today, you can learn anything your heart desires—online or offline. But you need to apply the information and convert it into useful knowledge. We didn't always talk about knowledge as having power in the workplace. In the days of the Industrial Revolution, it used to be that all you needed were your hands.

The modern world is different. In 1959, Peter Drucker coined the term "knowledge worker." He was referring to employees like you, employees of today, who make money not just because of what they do, but because of what they know. Your potential to learn is unlimited. Unlike the number of widgets you can make with your hands or sell in a given day, there is no limit to how much you can know. You can always learn more.

We don't always recognize the power of knowledge. Instead, we are held back by assumptions and beliefs that aren't always true. One of these dogmas is the belief that if you don't have a college degree, you are doomed forever. This is not only untrue, but also dangerous to anyone who aspires to move up in the world. If you have a job, or if you have ever had a job, you know it's not about a college diploma. It's about the value you bring, yourself, with or without a degree. All you need to apply the strategies and concepts in this book is a deep desire to better your financial situation for you and your family and the understanding that your dreams and desires can only flourish with information and knowledge.

When I speak to audiences, I often ask, "What is the difference between a person who makes $250 a week and one who makes a million dollars?" The answer I immediately hear is that the difference is that one is poor and the other is rich. I tell them that being rich or poor doesn't have anything to do with it. Their eyes light up when I tell them that the difference is simply information.

The person who is making a million dollars a week knows things that the person making $250 doesn't. He knows things that are worth money, and that people are willing to pay for.

The first Enlightenment was about knowledge and information, opening the eyes of the people so that they could free themselves from superstition and the limits of faith-based beliefs and actions.

This second Enlightenment is (in part) about liberation from the Industrial Revolution mindset that so many companies still practice today. These companies limit employees' access to riches—and thus they stand in the way of real personal development. The system is stuck in the past; however, the needs today are different. The world isn't just about creating human machines to be exploited by corporations; today's employees want more than just a salary to pay their bills and save a little. They also want to live, and a one-week vacation a year is not enough.

This Age of Enlightenment is about using your mind to create the life you desire. If you open your mind to the possibilities for raising your own salary in your work place, a brand new world will manifest in front of you. Cavemen didn't have this luxury. They lived by instinct alone. They lived in fear of nature's elements—elements we have brought under control because we applied our minds to them.

You have resources at your command right where you are, right inside your work place. Your employer can't keep you on a fixed salary if you bring your intellect into the equation. All you need to do is flip your mindset from passive to active, and from reactive to thinking, just like the people who started the first Age of Enlightenment. They liberated themselves from oppression and poverty, eventually leading to the French Revolution—a revolution that brought to humanity many of the benefits we enjoy today.

Go ahead. Look at your job—and shift! Shift the way you look at it! Max Planck, who won the Nobel Prize for Physics in 1918, said, "When we change the way we look at things, the things we look at change."

You have been conditioned to look at the world in a certain way, but you can choose to look at it in whatever way you want. Look at it in a way that gives you the power to earn raises beyond mere adjustments for inflation and the competitive salaries of the industry marketplace. Look at it in a way that can secure financial safety for you and your loved ones and gain promotions that do more than just feed your ego. Look at it in a way that can give you the flexibility to go on vacation whenever you feel like it. Look at it in a way that can free you from entrapment by the constraints of time and money.

I know, it sounds like a fantasy. But by the end of this book, you will realize that it can be your new reality. No business on the planet, regardless of the industry, is taking full advantage of all the resources available to them: staff, raw materials, equipment, products and services, customers, cash flow, connections, projects, and on and on and on. These excess resources are available for the taking. You can learn to capitalize on them and make them work for you.

If you decide to take advantage of the new opportunities you can create in your job, any amount of money you make will fall under one of three categories: 1) earned income, 2) portfolio income, or 3) passive income.

1. *Earned Income*: This is money generated by working. Your salary is considered earned income.

2. *Portfolio Income*: This is money generated by the selling of any kind of investment.

3. *Passive Income*: This is money generated with little or no effort at all. You get this money from assets or possessions you have bought or created. If you bring a new customer to your employer, you have created a new source of income for your company (or asset) and you should receive passive income from your one-time effort.

The beauty of becoming an employeepreneur is that you can also add the portfolio and passive income categories to the way you make money. Rich people always have multiple sources of income. Our time and energy is limited. We need to enlist systems to make money for us. Also, keep in mind that by using your employer's resources you are making money without any overhead or expenses to produce your new income.

You can turn your boss into an ally who will work on your individual projects, as long as they are still making money. You can do it. Your salary doesn't have to be limited, unlock your salary. Your new life is just a few short chapters away.

Chapter 5
From Employee to Employeepreneur

WHAT DOES IT TAKE?

The number one thing you need to become an employeepreneur is a job.

What if you don't have a job? These three tips will help you get one in your industry:

1. Identify ideal (or prospective) companies
2. Don't write a résumé—create a proposal!
3. Present yourself as well as you can, and leave your proposal with them.

Identify Ideal (or Prospective) Companies

Identifying and finding information about the companies you are interested in working for doesn't have to be difficult. Each industry has its own ways of doing things. Each has its own networking events, job boards, Internet sites, etc. The best place to find information about companies and be able to contact people in your industry today is LinkedIn (http://www.linkedin.com). This website can introduce you to everyone from the top CEOs to the lowest-level employees.

Once you decide which companies you might want to work for, you must research them and find out what is causing them pain. What are their biggest challenges? Take this information and create your own personal business proposal. Demonstrate your value by showing them the types of solutions that you will bring to their business.

Many companies are demanding duties beyond employees' job descriptions. If you come into a new job with new ideas and strategic suggestions, it will be easier to become an employeepreneur once you are inside because you will have a solid idea about how to sell your projects and ideas.

Don't write a résumé—create a proposal!

A proposal is a plan of action—and it doesn't just have to be words on paper. A proposal can be a video, a PowerPoint presentation, a written document, or any other form of presentation about you and your ideas for the business. Make sure that you make the proposal as dynamic and exciting as possible for your prospective employer to consider.

Present the information about you (that would normally appear on your résumé) in a different way. Make an impact. Don't talk only about what you did in the past—talk about the things you want to do in the future, and specifically the things you want to do for this employer. Let them know that you have researched them and have ideas about how your expertise can help them move forward. Use infographics whenever possible to illustrate your information. People are overwhelmed with too much written information and they are getting used to the graphical representation of the written word.

Human resources (HR) employees don't want to read long blocks of text anymore—use pictures, graphics, videos, or anything that allows you to communicate your value quickly and persuasively. If you present your personal and commercial proposal in this way, you will stay in your prospective employer's head for a long time, and even if you don't get this job, you might be hired in the future.

Many industries are struggling, and many people are looking for jobs. Companies want to hire only the best. You need to stand out and present yourself in a way that highlights the benefits you will be able to provide. You want to set yourself apart from all the other job seekers and show your prospective employer the value you can bring to his company.

If you don't know anything about shooting videos or creating PowerPoint presentations—learn! Every time you see a person who knows how to do something well, remember—she didn't always know how to do that! She had to learn to do it—and you can learn it too! You have the capacity to learn anything, as long as you set your mind to it.

Present yourself as well as you can, and leave your proposal with them

First, wear a suit and tie. Regardless of your industry, a good personal presentation is never out of fashion. Dress professionally. If you identified the right companies, did your research, and created your proposal, then all you need to do is present it to each of your targets. Make sure you make enough copies. Don't give it only to the Human Resources manager—he might not see the value. Give it to the sales manager as well—and the general manager, assistant general manager and everyone related to your expertise within the company.

Remember, the HR department does only what it is told to do—the executive management team controls the hiring. If you can present solutions (don't give them your whole ideas) to the business's hardest problems—often problems the HR management team may not know about—you can make the hiring process and decision easier for them and for you. Don't limit your chances by going only to the HR department, sometimes they don't know what they ought to be looking for.

If you can't meet in person with these managers, mail your proposals. If you can, send the DVD, CD, or written document via FedEx, UPS, or certified mail from the Post Office—this way you can be sure someone is actually receiving it. Whenever possible, bring your proposal in person to the offices of the companies you have selected. But don't limit your search to your city—in today's connected world, you can work from anywhere.

MAKING THE MOVE

If you already have a job, please understand that to make the mental move from employee to employeepreneur (and remember—this move isn't physical, it's mental), the first thing you need to understand is that you already possess everything you need to be an employeepreneur.

Becoming an employeepreneur involves three parts: (1) knowledge, 2) mindset, and (3) execution. You are employed because you know something and because you can do something with what you know. You have knowledge and you can execute. You are valuable to your boss because your knowledge and your execution are bringing revenue to his company.

In the usual employee role, when you do your job, you are doing the same thing as you could be doing as an employeepreneur, but you are getting a fixed amount of money from your employer and he receives most of the financial benefits of your actions.

All that's required from you to become a true employeepreneur is that you change the way you think about your job: a *mindset shift*. You need to understand that you are allowed to do more than what your job description entails. You are allowed to grow your role and become more valuable to your employer and your family.

The first step to change your situation is to look at your job as an assignment that is always changing and growing. Stop looking at it from a limited perspective. Look at it from the point of view of someone who could always find ways to be doing something more useful and more meaningful.

For example, if what you do helps people in any way, then start looking at the people who benefit from what you do. It doesn't matter if we're talking about a product or a service—you will always find new opportunities if you focus your attention on the end users and the processes used to deliver your product or service to them.

Your employer's customers are the ultimate recipients of what you do in your job. By focusing on them, the way they interact with you, and how they use your products and services, you can make a mental shift that will put you on the road to becoming an employeepreneur.

This mental shift is of major importance because you need to start seeing your role in a new light. This is the only way you can begin to discover that you can bring a lot more value to your employer's business and get paid more money for it.

To start the process of becoming an employeepreneur you only need to do three things:

1. Study your customers, business processes, and products and services;
2. Tell your boss that you want to grow;
3. Set up a "mental lab" in your current role.

Study your customers, business processes, and products and services

If you have been at your present job for at least six months or a year (or even a couple of months), you should have a solid understanding of what your company does. You should have a strong knowledge of who your customers are, the business processes used to deliver your products and services, what you sell, and the benefits you bring to the customers' lives.

This should be your starting point. Thinking hard about these aspects of your job will open doors that you never imagined, but you have to work at it. You have to look at your job with a new perspective, as if your employer's customers were your own customers. In some ways, this should not be hard to do because you serve them every day. In other ways, it can be difficult because it requires forcing yourself to look beyond your usual patterns of thought. But remember that practice makes perfect.

If you work in direct contact with customers, then you have a fairly good idea of who they are. You know how often they visit the business, what they buy and how often, and what their biggest needs are.

Many businesses use processes that are outdated or could simply be better. If you start looking at these processes with your employeepreneur eyes, you will discover flaws in how the service is delivered and how you address the customers' biggest challenges. Once you start looking closely, ideas, concepts, and opportunities should come to mind.

Pay attention to what you sell. Talk to the customers and listen to what makes them dissatisfied or frustrated. Don't look at these customers as complainers—look at them as idea generators. Look at them as your new partners! They bring new opportunities for you to make money. All you need to do is find solutions to their problems.

You need to find connections. Look at how the different departments operate to put a customer in front of you. You need to look at the entire structure of the company—the marketing department, the sales department, the kitchen, the security staff, the IT department, the finance department—everyone.

The people who work in these departments are your co-workers—talk to them. Ask them questions.

Find out all you can about what they do, and where their pain points are. Go beyond your job description.

Tell your boss that you want to grow

Set up a meeting and make sure that you prepare for it. Employees reaching out because they want to personally grow and improve their performance—that's something that most business owners and managers have experienced. However, you will be changing the game plan. They may be confused or intrigued at first. Your main challenge will be to clarify that you want to expand your role without impacting your current obligations. You want to do more, and you want to help the business grow.

Tell your employer that you will not let any of your new ideas hurt your required role. Perhaps during your work hours, you would promise not to engage in any activities related to bringing new business to the company. All of your extra activities will be conducted before and after your work hours. Your employer pays you for the time you're at work—she will want you to perform your job duties during those times.

Don't disclose any of your ideas in the first meeting. This meeting is just to discover if your boss is on board with your employeepreneur plan. At the end of the meeting, you can expect one of two reactions: "sorry, you can't do that," or "sure, how can we start?"

Be prepared for either response. Let's expand a little on the two possible reactions.

"Sorry, you can't do that."

This reaction is typical and you shouldn't be surprised if it happens. You have to be very careful how you proceed from here. If you try to push it, you will be seen as a problem and your ideas will be rejected completely. If you mention that you will bring your ideas to the competition, it may also sound like you are trying to threaten your boss.

"Sorry, you can't do that" shouldn't be a reason for you to give up. On the contrary, it should be a reason for you to open yourself to new possibilities. Keep your current job, but grab a directory and start looking for other companies in your industry that would put greater value on your expertise and innovative ideas—and be open to letting you use your job as a source of income and a source of problem-solving to increase your salary.

The sad truth is that many business owners are comfortable with the way their businesses are running and they don't want to rock the boat. Your boss may be worried about his own job. Research a few other companies in your industry and approach them with your ideas for new products, services, and innovations. Test the waters. See if they could use your help in finding new customers, or making current customers more satisfied.

Make sure to protect yourself with non-disclosure agreements (NDAs) and carbon copy (cc:) emails to a trusted friend to make sure you have proof of any interaction. Consult a lawyer just to be safe. If your employer is not on board with your ideas, putting the plan into action is a little more difficult, but not impossible. Don't give up!

"Sure, how can we start?"

This is another possible scenario, and you should be prepared for it too. You have to make it easy for your boss to accept your proposition. This means you have to assume all of the risk involved in the execution of your new projects.

The first statement out of your mouth should be, "I only get paid extra if I get results for the business." They will love this because it takes away all of the risk for them. Now they know that you will work your heart out to generate new revenue for the company.

With this step out of the way, you can proceed to explain how you will protect the company's brand, reputation, and customers, and you will only undertake initiatives that will help your employer.

Set up a "mental lab" in your current role

Employers hire people for two reasons: their current skills, and their capacity to learn. Your current skills are what get you the job, but your potential to learn and adapt is what allows you to keep the job. Each time your boss sends you to a conference, training course, or even simply engages you in a brainstorming session, he is using your potential to learn new skills in order to increase profit for the company. He's using your mental lab.

A lab, as you may already know, is a testing site. Make your job your new testing site. Make it a place where you will form connections between disparate ideas in order to develop new concepts. Everything should be looked at as part of an experiment. Customer complaints should be welcomed, errors should be analyzed, and nothing should be overlooked.

Be sure to carry a pen and paper with you throughout the day to record new insights. Alternatively, use your cellular phone to type notes, which you can email to yourself at the end of each day.

Additional Concepts to Keep in Mind

There are a few other important things to keep in mind as you make the shift from employee to employeepreneur.

Your company's objectives and goals

If you know your company's objectives and goals, you will be in a better position to participate in your company's vision of the future, and help them achieve their goals.

For instance, if you know that your company is approaching a financial milestone, you can use this information as you look for ways to pitch customers or present your new projects.

Companies love milestones. Investors demand that milestones be reached at all costs—even if the company has to lay off workers, sell defective products (which they may even have to recall later), or give away inventory at a discount.

If you know what's going on with the company, from a larger perspective, you can use this information for your benefit. Information, as always, is the key. Connect with the people in your company who can make key information available to you. To be in the know is to be in the money. Be in the money.

You can have other people help you as you prepare projects for your employer, but don't let them take control. Make them part of your team, but don't bring them into the deals you make with your employer. The knowledge and perspective of other individuals at your company (and outside of your company) can be invaluable. If you think that you hold all the answers, you are limiting yourself.

Customer service: a new perspective

Every customer you bring to your employer's business can become your customer for life. Treat your customers like kings and queens.

Always remember that if you do a good job taking care of their needs, they can bring not only financial benefits to you and your employer, but also open new opportunities and even markets in other regions. If they want to buy other products and services from your company or other companies, they can also use your services, and you can benefit greatly from a good customer relationship, especially if your customer is not familiar with your region and you are his only contact.

Try to arrange for the best customer service agents to handle the accounts of your personal customers. Make it clear that your customers are VIPs and should be treated with the utmost deference.

Your boss's reputation and status

Remember that your boss's reputation is on the line when he allows you to pursue your employeepreneur ventures. Respect your boss and always remember that he gave you the opportunity to become an employeepreneur. (Remember this especially when you start to make more money than he or she does!)

Don't ever make him look bad. Keep your promises and conduct yourself with humility and an understanding of your co-workers and your role as an employee—assuming you even need to remain an employee after you start applying all these strategies in depth.

Deleting yourself from the equation

Forget about yourself. Look to help everyone around you. Try to find ways that you can help everyone who comes in contact with you. Believe it or not, this will help you make even more money.

Your problem-solving skills will develop to such a degree that solving problems for your company—and for people in general—will become second nature.

New schedule: three days a week—or two?

Once your efforts start paying off, you can modify your work schedule to fit your lifestyle. Remember to stay humble and obey your company's rules and policies.

Creating value

What is value? Let me give you an example. I am teaching business to my two young sons and I often talk to them about value. I tell them a story to illustrate what I mean. Imagine two apple salesmen—

Salesman A and Salesman B— selling apples side by side in a market. They set their apples on their tables, display their prices (a dollar per apple), and sit down to wait for customers. They have good days and bad. The business earns enough for them both to get by and cover their basic needs.

However, one day, Salesman B begins to wonder how he can make more money than he's making now. His wife is pregnant and his family will need a bigger home after the baby is born. Although Salesman B is making money, it's barely enough to cover all of his expenses, both business and personal. He can't increase his inventory because there's not enough profit, and he can't increase the price of his apples because of the competition.

He decides to find the solution within the product itself: the apples. He starts learning about presentation and how it affects the value a customer perceives in the product. He learns about instant gratification and how people perceive ready-made food to be more appealing. He learns about giving customers as many options as possible in order to make them feel more in control of their purchase.

Armed with all of this new knowledge, he starts to put his plan into practice. The next day, transformation complete, he goes to the market to sell. His table is the same, and he's the same person, but his strategy has changed completely. Now he is displaying four options instead of one:

Product #1: Sliced and peeled apples, arranged nicely on small plastic plates that he bought in bulk for two cents each. He puts slices of lemon next to the plates, to make it prettier, and add perceived value. The lemons are an optional choice. The customer can decide if he wants them. The price for this product is two dollars. One dollar for the apple, and one dollar for the plate, the slicing, and the presentation—and that second dollar is almost entirely profit.

Product #2: A combination of two apples—one sliced and peeled, and the other left whole, along with a plastic knife he purchased in bulk for only one cent each. Including the plastic knife gives the customer the option of peeling the whole apple later. For this added value—the sliced apple, plus the whole apple, and a knife—he charges $2.75.

Product #3: The original whole apple, but also including a knife and slice of lemon. For this product, he charges $1.50—mere pennies spent, translating into fifty cents of added revenue.

Product #4: The original product (just an apple) without any added value. But with so many more options than his competition, he decides to raise his price and charge $1.20 for the very same apple. Why? He is now positioning himself as a fancier, customer-focused business.

What happened here? Salesman B didn't go out and buy expensive equipment or a special apple peeler. He peeled the apples with a knife. He bought plates, knives, and lemons. Innovation (the twin sister of marketing) is free. Human imagination and ingenuity come naturally to every human being. The key is to give yourself permission to act and to make bold changes in your commercial and personal life.

Why did Salesman A stay with his old business model? Because it was safe. He knew the outcome. But, most of all, it was his personal mindset that made him stay with the same model and never innovate. He was used to the results he was getting and he was content to stay where he was. But once customers saw the new offerings of Salesman B, it was not good news for the future of Salesman A.

Any business, in any industry, must always work to increase value. Value increase is why people start businesses in the first place. They want to increase the value of their lives. They want to have more control, and make more money. Most likely, you started working for your current employer to have more control over your finances and make more money. But right now, most likely, you are doing a repetitive task that generates a repetitive salary. Please understand that your *value creation* is your exchange currency. The value you can produce from your mind is what you will exchange for hard currency or money with your employer. You have boundless value inside and all around you. Ralph Waldo Emerson said, "What lies behind us and what lies before us are tiny matters compared to what lies within us."

Value creation is the only thing that will allow you to raise your own salary. Your boss or employer wants to see the money coming in and his customers want to see the value offered to buy more. You have to create that value. You can do it. You are a creator. Create what other people need or want and you will have everything you desire for you and your family.

Value is the only reason the customers keep coming

back to your employer's business. They want to receive more benefits and value-added solutions. They want to improve their lives. If your employer stops improving their lives, he or she will certainly go bankrupt.

Creating value is about never settling for what's already there. You can always make things better for your employer's business and make more money while doing it.

One more story about my youngest son. I watch the television show "Shark Tank" with my two children each week. On each episode of "Shark Tank," entrepreneurs seek money for their businesses or startup companies from five wealthy investors. The show is full of valuable insights, and I like discussing each episode with my children as we watch. My goal is to teach them lessons about what it means to be an entrepreneur. After watching the show one night, I showed them an old commercial about drugs—the one where a man pretends that your brain is an egg and drugs are the hot oil in a pan. He breaks the egg and puts it in the pan to fry, saying, "This is your brain on drugs."

That same night, we also talked about the dangers of smoking cigarettes. I went online and showed them pictures of two sets of lungs: one healthy, from a non-smoker, and the other from a smoker, blackened and diseased. We finished the discussion, and then I told them to brush their teeth and get ready for bed. A few minutes later, I went into their bedroom to make sure they were ready to go to sleep. I saw my youngest son coming out of the bathroom with tears in his eyes and sobbing. I asked him what happened and he said, "I don't want you to die. I love you so much," with tears flowing down his cheeks.

Somehow, the lessons I was teaching my son made him feel an appreciation for the value I can bring to his life as an adult, by teaching him valuable lessons for his future. The value and love he saw in what I was doing for him made him cry, for fear that one day he would lose me.

Can you ever make the kind of impact in the life of a customer that they will be moved to tears for fear that they will lose you as a service provider? Probably not—but you can strive to come close. How can you make yourself more and more important to your employer's customers? How can you show them how much you appreciate them, and give them reason to appreciate you?

The answer is simple: bring value to their lives. This can sometimes be easier than you think. Concentrate on giving. I don't mean giving your ideas away without receiving anything in return. I mean that you should focus your attention on making your employer's business more prosperous and profitable by adding tremendous value in all possible areas. If you focus your attention this way, you will see new opportunities wherever you turn.

Banish the thought of competition from your mind, and simply focus on value. You can add value to everything you touch, every person you meet, and every situation in which you find yourself.

A few years ago, I went to a talk by Howard Schultz, the CEO of Starbucks, as he launched his book *Onward* at Florence Gould Hall in New York City. I met a woman who was the owner of an online video business teaching people how to present themselves well on television. I started offering her ideas on how she could expand her business on a global scale—ideas she had never thought of, because she did not have the outsider's perspective that I did. She got very excited and said, "Wow! I didn't come to see him, I came to see you!" The kinds of feelings you get from interactions like that are worth more than money. Give, give, give—and it will all come back to you, multiplied many times over.

Chapter 6
Case Study: Discover How I Raised My Own Salary At My Job By 84%. I Used 4 Skills You Use Every Day!

Instead of writing this report, I wish I could go out on the street, walk up to you and alert you about the risks and rewards the job market holds for you. However, I know you would think I am crazy and dismiss any hair-on-fire warning from me.

Having a job today represents a blessing and risk for you and your family. If you have been watching the current trends in the job market, you know that jobs are facing the greatest threat in history. It's not only your co-worker who wants your position or the next promotion anymore.

Today the threats are not so easy to fight. Now, it's Artificial Intelligence, Robotics, Algorithms, outsourcing (local and abroad), mergers and acquisitions, lay-offs, sickness, cheaper employees, software, globalization, a teenage disruptor, etc.

The list is endless. Adding insult to injury is the fact that most employees −in different industries − have not gotten a salary raise in years. And when they do, it's usually to catch up with inflation. It seems that there is nothing you can do to stop the machine's attack.

You know how to act when the attack comes from an aggressor co-worker, but how can you protect your job from the inner workings of an algorithm, or software? "The best defense is a good offense," they say in sports...and it's true.

It's really amazing how, even in the most hopeless situations, we can be victorious. I can tell you that your best defense is not working more to please your boss, getting to work on time or even surrendering to the *** kissing demands of the corporate world to win favor. All that can help, but it can only take you so far.

No one can save your job from these kinds of threats - not your boss, not even your employer - because no one is safe. However, you have many options. You can get a new job, open a business, or do nothing, which is also always a choice. Regardless of your decision, it's vital to understand what your position is in the bigger picture.

What is your position? Your position is a job. A job is a limited set of tasks you do every day. That limited set of tasks determines your salary and your leverage at work. To survive (and even thrive) in the upcoming job onslaught, you must become a Jobpreneur. Jobpreneurs are CEOs in disguise. They are CEOs of their jobs.

They disrupt their companies from the inside out. They raise their own salaries because they know that no one is going to raise them for them. Your job has wealth in it, if you open your eyes and start HACKING. This report is about showing you how I raised my own salary at my job. This is the door - now you have to walk through it to start raising your own salary.How Did I Do it?

I got my job in December 2016 and, by mid-March 2017, I had already convinced my boss to pay me $25,000 to help the business attract and engage more customers. This was not luck or happenstance.

This was the result of the application of 4 specific skills that you possess and use every day. I will walk you through the 4 skills, or strategies, so that you can pick up on the main concept of becoming and acting like a jobpreneur to raise your own salary.

How Did I Do it?

I got my job in December 2016 and, by mid-March 2017, I had already convinced my boss to pay me $25,000 to help the business attract and engage more customers. This was not luck or happenstance.

This was the result of the application of 4 specific skills that you possess and use every day. I will walk you through the 4 skills, or strategies, so that you can pick up on the main concept of becoming and acting like a jobpreneur to raise your own salary.

The First Day of Work:

The first day of work, Joanna tried to clean my desk, but I gently took the spray and cleaning rag from her hand and proceeded to clean my own desk. I was just doing what I felt was right and, without even knowing it, I was positioning myself as someone who took initiative.

Remember, I wrote the book, but I was not active on it; I didn't even read the book. It scared the living Buddha out of me. If I opened it and started to read, I immediately started editing it all over again! So the book's content was not so fresh in my mind. However, I was behaving as a Jobpreneur.

After I got hired and I started to work in the office, I started noticing a lot of opportunities to make money as a Jobpreneur, but I was too new to introduce myself as a Jobpreneur, a concept not many business owners are familiar with.

Instead of talking about my intentions, I decided to give the book to my boss as a gift and see what happened. She liked the book very much, and I asked if I could give a copy to all my co-workers. She said it was okay and I gave everyone a copy, for free.

This is how I introduced myself softly as a Jobpreneur without causing too much disruption in my new job with this new concept. I suggest you do the same. Introduce yourself as a Jobpreneur, but do it softly. Don't make a fuss. There are big egos in the corporate world. Don't scare them.

It can be as simple as saying to your boss/employer: "I am reading an article about being a Jobpreneur... a Jobpreneur is an employee who decides to help his employer to _____. "What's your take on that?" Then listen as if your life depended on what she'll say next.

Okay, back to my story: From the moment I started working there, I wanted to become a resource for everyone. Some of my co-workers read the book and told me they liked it and some didn't read it. But it didn't matter if they read it or not - the important thing is to contribute to the growth of others (as I'll explain later in this report).

I started working as an employee and then transitioned into a Jobpreneur. The difference between the two is the value you bring as one or the other. Obviously, a Jobpreneur brings more value to the table. As a Jobpreneur, you elevate yourself to the unofficial position of CEO.

Think about it. A CEO's job is to use all resources available in the company to increase profits, and, as a Jobpreneur, you would do the same. In the early developing stages of this concept, I used the word Employeepreneur to define what I call today a Jobpreneur.

In this image, you can see an employeepreneur slightly above the boss.

1- Helping The Company Increase Profits

If getting more sales or customers is not in your job description, this could be an area where you could increase your salary. Trust me; your boss doesn't know everything. Most companies today are terrified of the future. Today, any 15-year old teenager can disrupt or destroy an industry, let alone your company. This is how I increased my salary - by presenting my boss with a project to get more customers.

2- Reducing Operation or Overhead Costs

Any employee can help the company reduce costs if they keep their eyes open. Let me tell you a little story about saving money for the company. An employee from the matches company Swan saw an opportunity to save money for the company and also to make some money for himself.

He approached management and said: "If I can show you a way to save millions of dollars and it works, would you give me a portion of the savings?" The company said, "Yes," so he organized a meeting with the company's management and his lawyer and introduced his idea. Protect yourself, always.

He told them: "You're spending a lot of money by putting the sand paper on both sides of the box of matches. Put it only on one side." This simple idea saved the company millions over the years and helped this employee increase his salary beyond his wildest imagination.

3- Creating New Products And Services

The company you work for right now was once a simple idea. Don't let the expensive suits or shiny shoes your boss and CEO wear fool you. That little idea supports their life style. You have many ideas every day. Your ideas could increase the company's bottom-line and you could increase your salary, if you become a Jobpreneur, without causing friction among your co-workers and superiors.

You know what your company offers; you know the products and services. If you happen to go on vacation and you meet a great potential buyer, ask your boss:

"Hey, if an employee brings in a million dollar buyer, can he get a commission on the deal?" But! Before you do that, please test the waters. Corporations behave like if you belonged to them... that would include your ideas.

This is why asking a casual question, or making a casual comment about reading an article or I saw this book title, like my book for example: Job, Inc., is always a good idea. Pay attention to what is going on with your industry. Products and services spring from the needs of people, not from the directives of executives.

Ideas are free! Well, that's not true, it takes a little effort, but it's worth it. You're reading this report, I'm certain you know that.

Okay, now that I briefly introduced you to the main ways to make more money at your job, let me show you the 4 skills or strategies I used to increase my salary at my job. These skills are natural in all of us and they can work for or against us. It all depends on how we use them.

Okay, here we go:

Skill #1: Your Ego

We hear people talk about the ego all the time but few people ever talk about the feeding mechanism our ego uses to grow and get stronger every day. I thought about it and I realized that our ego is created from our senses. Think about it.

The simplest way to explain the Ego is by saying that the Ego is a sense of SELF. How do we create our sense of self? Through information. How do we capture that information that creates our social-selves? Using our senses!

Namely: Sight, Smell, Touch, Taste and Hearing. This is a system of search. This system is always in search mode. The search is named: **WIIFM or What's in it for me?**

This is the way our ego is created. This is how we form our sense of identity; it's through our senses. This is the mechanism that protects us and alerts us of any imminent danger. It's always scanning the environment for what's useful for us. However, its original purpose was to sniff dangerous predators in the jungle, it's original use is ineffective today.

Okay, now, **how did I use this skill to raise my salary?** Well, this is the way to start becoming a Jobpreneur without causing friction.

All we have to do is simply flip the function of the

Ego from WIIFM to **WIIFT, or What's In It For Them?** The core foundation of this concept is knowing that there's no lack in the universe. If you can fix in your mind that wealth comes ONLY from three places: 1) people 2) nature and 3) ideas, then you will understand that *you are value and that there's no lack in the universe.*

I flipped my Ego (WIIFM) by simply helping anyone I met to grow two inches before they left my presence. Believe me, it's easier than you think. **All you can give someone is information**. Information became my most previous gift to give to people with whom I came in contact. Whenever I helped someone grow two inches, I grew 6, 12, 20. Whatever you put out into the universe comes back to you multiplied.

So many people are suffering because they lack simple knowledge of the mind, so I would help them with simple stuff like: "Your thoughts are only visitors requesting a meeting with you, don't be afraid of them." I am a student of metaphysics and the power of the mind and subconscious. It just fascinates me!

So, there you have it, strategy #1. Please don't believe or disbelieve me - use it!

I flipped my Ego and used its ability for the benefit of my co-workers and customers. It's a natural tendency that you just have to redirect. Simple.

Skill #2: Wealth Consciousness

You are wealth. You are aware of wealth; however, if you're not experiencing wealth at this moment, it's because you are more aware of something else: *Lack of wealth Consciousness.*

Please understand this, the systems of society of the world are built on a lack of consciousness. The economists create lack of resources. The school system creates lack of initiative, creativity and self-esteem. The job system creates and perpetuates lack of prosperity. The health system creates lack of health consciousness. The news creates lack of peace and harmony. Everything around you creates lack of, lack of wealth and this way your value (and my value) creation is diminished systematically.

However, we are children of light. I am not talking God or religion here. I am talking science. I am talking Quantum Physics. This is all documented knowledge about not who we are, but what we are. What we are is more important than who we are. Who we are is just a bundle of emotions and information. What we are is power and God-like divinity (please replace God with Buddha, Allah or whatever god name you prefer).

So, our societies force us into lack of consciousness; however, we feel a natural and powerful inclination towards wealth consciousness but we have forgotten because all we see is lack. If you start practicing wealth consciousness - flipping your Ego, for example - you will start to see value or wealth everywhere. This is why step #1 is so important. Don't believe that if you help someone at your job with some information you're going to lose or not get what you desire - there's enough for everyone.

So, practicing wealth consciousness is simply being aware of wealth. It's knowing that it's everywhere you look. You can see it in your own house, you can see it on the street, you can see it in people, in nature and in your ideas. Please don't let society confuse you when it comes to wealth and money. Money is nothing more than a reflection, a tiny aspect of wealth. Wealth is the real deal. Wealth is the core center where you want to operate from everyday of your life.

Wealth is:

Feeling healthy from a vegan diet or balanced eating
Having a lot of money to cover your needs and beyond
Loving someone feeling loved by (that) someone
A beautiful and soul elevating sunset
A shiny and luminous sunrise
A beautiful song you enjoy listening to
A nice trip with friends or family
A happy moment regardless of what's going on
A great idea to improve other people's lives
A nice dinner at a nice restaurant
A beautiful show on Broadway or any other theater strip
Being able to buy nice things for your wife, husband, girl/boyfriend
All this is wealth. Wealth is all the enjoyment you can derive from any activity. Sometimes money is necessary; sometimes it's not. Wealth is you. My kids and I always have discussions about price, value and products and services. I always tell them that nothing has price, nothing is expensive or cheap; things have value or they don't. Price is irrelevant, value is everything.
Price has nothing to do with value. We give value to things and then we pay for them in the agreed price. We are the value. My younger son Carlitos, he loves Lamborghinis. Sometimes he says, "Wow, they're

expensive!" and I am always quick to jump in and say: "Compared to what?"

I always tell him comparative stories about someone having to exchange his Lamborghini for a quarter to call his daughter because of an accident or eat a meal because she can't eat the car. This wakes him up to the fact that everything is based on value, not on price. So, create insane value for you and everyone around you - it's free. You don't have to pay for it. It's in the air, like Nikola tesla driving his car in New York with electricity from the ether, the air.

Capture value from people, nature and your ideas. Take it. Use it. Give plentiful to everyone around you and it will come back to you multiplied. Flip your Ego; it's the fastest way to go directly into wealth consciousness because the Ego is always looking for things you can use. The thing is that you can't pay yourself for the things that you find. You need people to pay you with the currency we use in society: money. When you make them grow 2 inches, you're adding real value to someone's life, value that someone will be willing to pay for, eventually.

I made sure that everyone with whom I came in contact walked away two inches taller: customer or co-worker. You don't have to be a genius. If you're reading a book and you find something amazing, give it away. If you have an insight about the job you do, share it. Never stop giving. I have some books left from my book selling days on Amazon, and I have this beautiful book for little girls (by the way, if you have a daughter - below 15 – and you're in New York and you want one, just let me know)...anyway, I digress.

I gave these books to my customers and co-workers

for their nephews, nieces and/or daughters. Become a giver and people will give back to you. This attitude helped me gain the trust and good will of everyone at my job. Please understand: this is not acting. If you don't genuinely like people and helping them grow, don't waste your time with this information. It's not going to help you.

Also, please understand that you have to grow as a person. Reading is the best way to acquire new information quickly. Watch videos on websites like Fora. tv, Tedx, trendhunter.com, YouTube and many others. Do something original. I, for example, started reading and walking in my neighborhood (and other areas) whenever I needed to run an errand, or go take the train to pick up my kids from school. I've read entire books doing this, people look at me weird and sometimes comment, but I don't care.

I am using my walking time to learn. You may not be as extreme as I am, however, find your own corner, claim your own identity and defend it. Be weird a positive way, in a magical way. Create your own little world of learning and testing lab. These ideas, if you're not familiar with them, are expanding your mind into a new way to look at your job, embrace it and don't let go.

Skill #3: Positioning

Positioning! Wow! This is pure power. Positioning is who you are in the hearts and minds of people. If you think about it for a second, you'd realize that you're always positioning yourself with everyone you meet on a daily basis.

Think about great personalities of history: Mandela, Kennedy, Jesus Christ, Martin Luther King Jr., Nikola Tesla and Gandhi. All these great people positioned themselves as leaders of their different areas and people came to know them and accept them as consistent, inspiring, giving and, most of all, brave. No one asks you if that is really your positioning when you're acting in society. They just see, act and understand that that's who you are, that's the way you are, that's you.

Companies all over the world spend billions of dollars every year protecting, enhancing or embellishing their brands. Why do you think that is? It's all about perception. It's all about how you are seen in the minds and hearts of the people you want to influence. There's a famous phrase that goes like this: "There's no second chance for a first impression." It's true.

What most people don't know (including me, years back) is that we can engineer that first impression without any fraud, or misleading the people with whom we want to interact. If you are not truthful and genuine in that first impression, your true self is going to come out later on in your behavior. You can't escape yourself for very long.

You can let your positioning be random when you interact with people, or you can take control of it. You can be intentional about it, deliberate or just casual. Either way, you are going to get a result. Create your positioning. How do you want people to see you? I wanted people to see me as a resource at my job and I accomplished that by giving nonstop. When you position yourself like that, you become a 'sweet' person to be around.

People want to be around you; they want to be part of what you do. They know that you mean well; they trust you. They see you as transparent. No agenda. Never expect anything in return from the person you give to.

These strategies work; however, if no one likes you at your job, they will withhold information from you. They will not be as helpful with you as you expect and your idea may not go anywhere. Position yourself as a learning leader. Always say, I am a learning leader, I can only teach what I learn and practice myself. I am an advancing woman. I am an advancing man. I help everyone I meet grow 2 inches. I leave them better than when I met them. I am a force of nature for good in the lives of others, my own and my loved ones.

Skill #4: Becoming a Jobpreneur

Have you ever wondered: Why are we employees? Why are we forced to wake up early in the morning and spend eight or ten hours stuck in an office or other location doing things that we might love but, most likely, we hate? Remember schools, they are just the forerunners to jobs.

Millions of people from all over the world go to work every day. Many of these people love what they do, many dislike what they do. Some jobs are boring; other jobs are interesting. Regardless of people's opinions, there's wealth in those jobs because you can find the three things that create wealth: people, ideas and nature.

Okay, we got that part clear. Now, how do you become a Jobpreneur? Simple. It's a mind-shift. You decide to become one. It's like being happy. You just decide to be happy and then all sorts of happy memories start to flow through your mind or exciting activities start to pop up in your head. Things you can do to continue to be happy; however, happiness started within you, without you needing anything from the outside.

Okay, but what is it that you decide to do? You decide to start looking at your job as a place where you can create value beyond your job requirements: remember - the three areas to add value to your employers' company so that you can make more money:

1- Helping the company increase profits
2- Reducing operation or overhead costs
3- Creating new products or services
These are the areas that you start looking at, just like the CEO of the company. You don't need permission; however, you need to clear the way. You need to test the waters and see how the company feels about that. They need your help and your co-workers help. They won't tell you because of pride or hierarchical crap, but they need your help like never before.

Remember, your raw material is ideas. You have ideas all day long. All you need is a system and this report has put one in your hands. You have also joined our community of Jobpreneurs to stay in the loop; that's good. If you start writing ideas, combinations of ideas, concepts, etc., you could come up with an idea that could potentially save your company, or make you a millionaire. **How cool would that be?!**

Here are some tips to help you along the way:
When your co-workers complain about something, listen, take mental notes, scribble down whatever ideas may come out of that complaint. Think solutions! Think about specific problems the company has and put your subconscious mind to work. Companies are recognizing the warning signs, so to speak. Many companies are even outsourcing their R&D (Research and Development) departments. If you visit a website named: www.innocentive.com. You'll find many companies that can't solve their problems internally and go to this open source problem solving website to find help. Did you read that? Read it again! That's proof that you have a great opportunity in your hands if you use these principles I am presenting to you today.

There are many new technologies your employers may not know about. They don't know everything. You might even find products or services from other industries that might enhance your company's products or competitiveness in the marketplace. There's no limit to the possibilities when you open your mind to the concept of being a Jobpreneur.

Please Note:

These strategies and concepts are only as good as your relationship with people. These are people's strategies, not technology or techniques. They don't work if there's no trust, integrity and honesty.

As you can see, these skills or strategies are natural to us. We use them all on a daily basis; it's just a matter of redirecting their use or learning a few concepts.

Positioning: you do it everyday. Now all you need to do is become deliberately aware and position yourself.

Your Ego: Redirect its natural inclination. Trust me on this; you'll thank me later. You do the Ego thing every day, too. It just doesn't serve you well when all its focus is on you. You don't have to run away from predators anymore. Upgrade your ego!

Wealth Consciousness: You are nothing but wealth, value and pure potentiality to create wealth. Become conscious of it! Stop looking at lack!

Becoming a Jobpreneur: It's all about thinking, which you do every day, too. Find new ways to use your mind, it helps to get into the Jobpreneur mindset. Remember, being a Jobpreneur is a mindset.

So, there you have it. Use me as a resource to grow. Allow me to help you grow 2 inches or more. Email me anytime with your questions.

Chapter 7
Creating Your Influential Team

THE TEAM

The last 50 years of human experience have dramatically increased our potential to create and innovate. In these last five decades, there have been more advances—in all areas of life, personal and professional—than in the 200 years prior.

Depending on the company you work for, the products and services your employer offers may range from selling ice cream to providing military mental health services, and everything in between. Your employee-preneur venture, whatever it is, will open up a world you never thought possible. This new world will expand the walls of your imagination and confront you many times with the fact that you don't have all the answers for the many questions your venture will face.

You may have many skills, but you may also be lacking some others that you vitally need. Your employer or boss may not be helpful in filling in the gaps. She might be busy with her own job duties, and will want to see a completed product or a tested idea before you present it. For this and many other reasons, you will need a team of people you can rely on.

Going from idea to creation can be daunting. Having ideas and not knowing how to bring them to life can be frustrating. Today, any project can take more skills and experience than you have. So many things we do each day are highly complex—sometimes it is hard even to turn on a TV using a remote control.

Today, there are so many possible approaches to everything we do that sometimes we can suffer from choice paralysis. You can have a great idea, but if you don't research the subject, and your presentation is not fluid, the idea can end up in the trash.

To be able to bring your ideas and innovations to life, you will need to rely on a team of professionals who can help you not only with presentations, public speaking, coaching, and developing your ideas and concepts, but also with your personal life.

These are a few keys to creating your team.

Experts

You need to know if someone has the qualifications you need for your project. If they don't have a portfolio, it could mean they don't take their profession seriously. This means they may not take your project seriously either. These experts will help you develop and put together your projects and ideas.

Check references

This seems to be a no-brainer, but you would be surprised how many people hire designers, editors, copywriters, and others without checking their references. When problems start showing up it is the first thing that comes to mind: "I should have checked their references."

Non-disclosure agreement

Use an NDA whenever possible. An NDA is an agreement you make with the expert who will perform work for you. This is an agreement to protect your ideas and concepts. Protecting your ideas is another reason you should check references—if someone's references have good things to say, it is an indication this person will not likely try to do anything illegal with your intellectual property.

Project description

If you can't meet in person with a potential team member, make a video describing what you need. If you can't shoot a video, write down your project description and use images (pictures, infographics, etc.) to be as clear as possible. Most problems between customers and experts result from a lack of communication and full understanding of expectations.

FINDING EXPERTS

The world has become a connected marketplace. Today you can find many professionals by just sitting in front of your computer. You can choose to work with professionals in your own country or other regions of the world. It can often be cost-effective to work with talented professionals in developing nations where labor is less expensive than it is in Europe, the US, or Canada.

There are some very good websites on the Internet that you can use to find the experts who can help you develop your ideas.

Elance
www.elance.com

This company acts as a broker between you and skilled professionals to ensure that the transaction takes place without any conflicts. These are some of the professionals you can find on the Elance website: editors, programmers, website designers, writers, marketers, website creators, consultants, and mobile developers (among others).

You don't have to pay Elance for connecting you with the experts—they take their fees from the expert's earnings. Elance protects you by putting your money in escrow. You release the funds only when you are satisfied with the work.

Odesk
www.odesk.com

Works in a similar way to Elance.

YouTube
www.youtube.com

YouTube can be very useful when you're looking for an expert. Many people on YouTube help others by creating videos that teach a variety of different subjects. These experts have reputations that they need to maintain in order to get more business. YouTube also has a section where you can leave comments about the experts. We are living in a time where reviews and references have become a driving force for new customer acquisition. Reputation, therefore, becomes more and more important for businesses and individuals every day.

Skype
www.skype.com

Skype is a free online communication platform that allows you to talk to anyone connected to the Internet, with a computer, mobile phone, or tablet. Skype also allows you to share your screen with other people. This is ideal for show-and-tell when communicating with your team. You can also find professionals on Skype by typing keywords in the contact search section.

Google+
plus.google.com

Works in a similar way to Skype.

As you grow your new employeepreneur venture, your ideas and innovations will also grow. Your team needs to keep pace with the new skills and expertise your growth will demand. Try to get referrals for other experts from within your network. This will minimize your exposure to experts with bad reputations.

If you are like me, you will try to learn as many skills as possible, and do as much of the work yourself—but you won't be able to master everything. The sooner you create your team, the sooner your concepts, ideas, projects, and innovations will expand—when you are able to incorporate other people's input, the vision will only grow.

MENTORS AND COACHES

All of these professionals and tools will prove to be very helpful in your new employeepreneur venture. But the people around you (family, friends, and co-workers) are also part of your team because they contribute to your personal mindset. They are part of the total package that forms your character and personality. If you tell your immediate circle about what you are trying to do to increase your salary, most likely they will laugh at you. Some will see the logic, but many will not, and you could easily get discouraged.

To prevent that from happening, you need mentors. Mentors are people who you purposefully choose to teach you something that you want to learn. They are the ones you go to when you have a burning question to which you can't find an answer. Mentors are helpful in so many ways—if we didn't pass knowledge from one to another we would still be in the Dark Ages.

One of the most powerful reasons we need mentors is because they take us from where we are to where we want to be. Your circle of friends, family, and coworkers are keepers of the status quo. They are there to ensure that you don't step out of line. If you try to stand out and claim your right to individuality and riches in the world, they may pull you back.

I remember telling a friend about my recent visit to the dentist. I made an appointment for 11:30am on a Monday. When I showed up for my appointment, I saw there were many other patients waiting. I approached the secretary's desk and said that I was there for my 11:30 appointment. She said, "Okay, take a seat." I asked, "When do I see the dentist?" She said, "Oh, you have to wait." I immediately said, "No thank you," and left the dentist's office.

My friend couldn't believe I did that to a dentist. She was surprised that I had behaved in such a way. Of course I was supposed to wait, just like all the other patients, even if I had an appointment for a specific time. But why shouldn't I try to find a dentist who respects my time just as I respect hers? I no longer talk to this friend about anything that indicates I am stepping out of line and not conforming to the herd mentality.

Your mentors will applaud this kind of behavior. They will encourage it, but not only that—they will also recommend a dentist who respects your time. Mentors are everywhere. You don't have to meet them in person. If you grab a book, buy a video, subscribe to their channels on YouTube, read their articles, or follow them on Twitter or Facebook, you are being mentored by their knowledge. In this way, you can have many mentors. But you also need some people you can go to with your own questions at any time. Access to smart, experienced mentors is key when it comes to developing ideas and innovations.

When you meet people you want to choose as your mentors, ask them. You'd be surprised how happy some people get when they receive such compliments. People are almost always happy to share knowledge. There's something gratifying about it. Some people will do it for free and others will charge. Pay for the service, and you will value it more. Paid coaches will teach you anything that you want to learn, and the payment creates a commitment that is very important to accomplish anything. A simple search on the Internet will give many results for coaches in your area. They are like magicians who can bring the best out of you. We are like mines that need to be drilled and dug up to extract the gold that lies hidden inside of us. Coaches and mentors are experts at doing just that.

The main difference between a mentor and a coach is intention. What is your intention when you look for help? What do you want to accomplish? A mentor is like a general practitioner. She will help you with general things in your personal and professional life. This person helps you achieve goals, assists with decision-making, and provides general guidance. A coach, on the other hand, is useful when you have a specific goal or need to improve a certain skill or set of skills.

Don't underestimate the power of having a mentor or a coach. They both can truly help you move closer to your goals and dreams.

Your employeepreneur venture will give you the money that you want and need to start living your dream life. When the money starts coming, you need people on your team who can help you deal with it and show you how to become financially literate with your newly acquired affluence.

Financial mentors and coaches can be lifesavers. If you follow the advice in this book, you will make more money. But you need to know how to protect it. When people tell me about all the things they would buy if they won the lottery, I always tell them that the first thing they should do is write a check to someone like Suze Orman, a major name in financial advising. I tell them that they need to buy financial advice. Track her down and give her your money. Contract her for two years of unconditional and open access.

I tell them that if they won the lottery and didn't seek financial advice right away, they could very quickly get back to the point where they need to buy lottery tickets again. The information and advice a good financial advisor can provide is truly invaluable. Find a good financial advisor who loves to teach. Make her part of your team. This person will open the doors to a brand new world in terms of growing and protecting your money. Learn about this world before you start making the big money.

Chapter 8
Personal Resources to Boost Your Salary

I gave a seminar in December 2011, in Times Square—in the heart of New York City—entitled "Resources to Money." I stated there that every person has resources at their disposal that they can use to create unlimited riches for themselves and for their families.

You may have heard that 5% of the world's population controls 95% of the world's money. But don't confuse money with wealth. Wealth is all around us and is available to everyone. I'll share a little secret: we all have wealth. Making money should not be the goal. The goal should be creating value—money will then follow. Money, you will realize, is merely a result of our actions and state of mind.

The truth is that every single one of us can be part of that 5% who have the money. I've come to realize that the reason the 5% control so much of the world's money is because they are the ones who truly understand that abundance is the result of ideas. But we all have ideas! If you ask my two sons where money comes from, they will point to their heads and tell you that it comes from ideas. There is a misperception about money among the 95%—a misperception learned from an early age when we go through the compulsory and archaic educational system. Our educational system is still based on the needs of the Industrial Revolution. Therefore, we learn that we can only make money within the constraints of our job descriptions.

We still have a system that teaches and promotes in children the mentality of a factory worker. We are taught to exchange time for money, when we should in fact be exchanging value and ideas for money. This is why becoming an employeepreneur is paramount to your success. You have all you need within your employer's premises to be successful.

Listen, you may be getting along just fine. You're paying your bills and maybe even saving some money. But is that all you want out of life? You wouldn't have bought this book if so. Your employer's business offers the perfect setup for you to operate. But to do it, you need to tap into your deeper self. You need to utilize all of your dormant resources—all of those personal qualities that are ignored by your current job description. You can use them to make your employeepreneur ventures grow with quantum leaps.

YOUR PERSONAL RESOURCES

You've likely heard a lot about personal resources, and the power that lies inside each one of us to achieve what we desire in life. But what exactly are these powers and how can we best use them? I would like to give you a short list of what I consider the most powerful characteristics that live inside of you, available at your command. This list represents some of the resources you can use to get anything you want in your life.

Thoughts

Your thoughts are electrical impulses that attract similar ones from the environment. Your life up to this very moment is the creation or manifestation of your thoughts. Guard your thoughts the same way that you protect a baby. Try to put only good thoughts in your mind. James Allen said, "As he thinks, so he is; as he continues to think, so he remains."

Desire

This is the seed that activates your dreams and moves you to take action. For your employeepreneur venture to take flight, desire always has to be present. If you don't have the desire to expand your ambition and create new products and services from your employer's resources, then nothing in this book can help you. But the mere fact that you bought this book and are reading it tells me that you want to succeed and that you are ready to do what is necessary.

Decisions

When I watched Bob Proctor open a seminar with the following declaration—"if you want to be rich all you need is to make a decision"—I suddenly understood the power of committing yourself to a dream or goal, along with a course of action. Your decisions move you in the direction you want to follow. If you make a decision and you commit to it, nothing is impossible to attain.

Action

Your actions will determine your outcome. Your actions are always the size of your dreams. If you have small dreams, your actions will be small and timid. If you have big dreams, your actions will be big, bold, and fearless.

Intention

Intention is a powerful force that, when aligned with your desires and actions, will provide clarity of purpose and eventually help you get what you want. Confused intentions can cause a lot of personal and professional pain, but when you are clear in your goals in every area of your life, you can proceed without doubts, and your actions can be in harmony with your innermost desires.

Attention

Whatever you pay attention to will expand and grow, regardless of what it is. Imagine that you are holding a magnifying glass in the bright sunlight and you are shifting its focus from one spot to another every ten seconds.

If you're trying to start a fire, but constantly focusing the sunlight on different spots, you will fail. Now imagine that you focus the magnifying glass on one single spot and don't move it an inch until you see a flame start to burn. This is a perfect example of the power of focused attention.

Energy

When you have the desire and the intention to do something, and then you focus your attention on it, your energy level sharply increases. You simply can't contain yourself. Energy is excitement, motivation, and life coming from inside of you. The human body is capable of superhuman feats when given enough reasons to unleash its greatest powers. Your energy level and enthusiasm will be determined by your aspirations. The best energy drink is a double dose of your vision or dream, when you wake up in the morning and when you go to bed at night.

Creativity

We are creative beings. We are always creating and recreating our lives through our thoughts and actions. The only limits to our creativity are the ones we impose upon it. You can apply creativity to your employeepreneur ventures and create amazing things if you follow these three helpful steps:

1. Look at what you do for your employer from the eyes of a stranger. What would a stranger change? What would he improve? What innovations would he want to see?
2. Write down any insights obtained while looking at your venture from this perspective.
3. Think about how you can implement these insights into your employeepreneur ventures to make them better. What do you need to do to make them happen? Do you have the resources or do you need to find a way to get them from the outside?

Ideas

Society has advanced immensely over time because our ideas have overcome many obstacles and solved problems that in the past hindered our progress. Your ideas are unique because you are unique. You have an unlimited supply of ideas that can produce the results you want in your life.

Express your ideas with clarity. Use pictures, graphics, and other tools to make them easy to understand and as compelling as possible. No one else sees the world the way you do. There is a software program called Mindjet that can be helpful in mapping your ideas. I use it and it helps me to clarify my thought processes immensely.

Awareness

Be aware! Many opportunities pass people by because they're not aware of their environments. Be present. Get out of the automatic ways of thinking and be exactly where you are, right now. Always pay attention to what is happening in your job and how your company is changing day to day.

Value-added Living

Put value into all of your actions, as well as into your work and your gifts to others. Only then will your life be filled with value and meaning. Every situation in life has inherent value that is revealed only when we open ourselves up to it. In your employeepreneur ventures, if you give enough value to your customers, you will have a true competitive advantage, capable of making you a leader in your company and your industry.

Knowledge

Knowledge is information that has been transformed into experience. Depending on your job, you will need to consume certain types of information. All of your actions are preceded by the information or knowledge you have. Read trade magazines, books, and articles about your job and your industry.

Learn as much as you can about marketing, sales, customer service, and business management. If you have a broad perspective about your industry, you will always find new projects to develop as an employee-preneur.

Attitude

This is a big one. Your attitude, more than any other personal attribute, will determine your future. Attitude refers to how you interact with life—how you accept what life throws at you and how you let the world flow through you—or how you resist the world and make your life hell for yourself and for everyone you come into contact with.

Your attitude determines how you take it when things don't go your way, and when life seems to be against you no matter what you do. Success and failure will come and go. You should always treat success and failure as strangers who can be on their way out of your life at any given moment.

Strength

One sentence: you are always stronger, faster, wiser, richer, and more resourceful than your circumstances. You have strength in you to overcome any situation you confront in your employeepreneur ventures. Never stop believing that.

Agreements

If you think that agreements aren't important, think about the monetary system in the world's economy. The only thing that keeps the world's economy intact is the fact that people all over the world agree to participate in it. We all agree that money has value.

If we didn't, the economy would fall apart. We exchange paper money—paper money that only has value because we all say it does—for actual products and services. The entire basis for the world's economy is a simple agreement.

Agreements are part of our lives, both personally and commercially. We agree to stop at traffic lights, and agree about whose turn it is to cross the street. We agree with our kids and our spouses about when and where to go on vacation, and we agree with our customers when they decide to use our services.

You participate in a silent agreement every time you go to a supermarket (or any store) and take something in exchange for money. The agreement is that what you are taking will satisfy your needs—and if it doesn't, you can get your money back.

Lawyers exist because agreements are broken on a daily basis. Honor your agreements and respect your customers. This is a basic principle for any business, especially an employeepreneur venture.

Inspiration

The word *inspiration* means to be in spirit and in harmony with what you desire in your life and with everything in existence. This is the state of mind in which millions of people find amazing ideas and concepts that make them rich. Be in spirit. Make inspiration your permanent state of mind.

Vision

Helen Keller said, "It is a terrible thing to see and have no vision." A vision is a mental image conceived and produced by our imagination. It is an image of our dreams and the things we desire to have in our lives.

What is the vision you hold in your mind for your employeepreneur venture? What is the life you want to create for you and your family? What do you see in that picture? Who is in that picture with you?

Character

Your character is the basis of your personality—and your employeepreneur venture is an expression of that same personality. Believe it or not, your venture will have a character and personality, just as you do.

Trust

You may hear a lot of people say, "I don't trust anyone." I believe that what they are really saying is that they are afraid. On both the conscious and subconscious levels, we are all trusting beings. We function in society because we trust. Everything we do is based on trust; even when we take all the precautions in the world, we are still counting on trust to enable us to move forward with our plans or our projects.

We trust that everything will go as planned even when it doesn't. We trust that the chef at a restaurant will cook tasty, safe food for us, and we trust our friends with our secrets. Trust enables us to accomplish things that we wouldn't otherwise be able to if we were paralyzed by fear.

These are all resources that are available to you. Use them, make them part of your employeepreneur venture and watch your venture as it grows to unimaginable heights.

Chapter 9
Raising Your Salary As Often As You Want

If you fix upon your consciousness the fact that the desire you feel for the possession of riches is one with the desire of omnipotence for more complete expression, your faith becomes invincible.
~Wallace D. Wattles

When it comes to your salary, disregard the chain of command that tells you that your boss has to make more money than you. A title that only inflates your ego doesn't help you pay your rent, pay for your kids' education, or pay for a fancy vacation. A raise that merely keeps pace with inflation is not a real raise. If inflation is 4%, and your raise is 4%, you are only staying even. It's not even a raise—it's a cost-of-living adjustment. And yet this is usually what you get when you ask your employer for a raise: *a long-overdue adjustment.*

For centuries, whenever an employee needed a raise or wanted to take a vacation, he had to go to his boss—and beg. Raises or inflation adjustments were often denied—for unjust reasons, or often for no reason at all—causing embarrassment, self-esteem issues, and a loss of self-worth. "I am not working hard enough," the employee would think. "I am not good enough." "I am simply not worth it."

Think about it: you were hired because you have some skills or expertise that your employer needed. Your skills grow on the job, whether through formal training or merely experience—and yet your salary never reflects that growth. Whatever your salary is right now as an employee, you could be earning double, triple, or quadruple that amount—and maybe even more. You have a set of skills that are needed in your industry. If you didn't, you wouldn't still have the job.

You can certainly use your expertise for your employer's benefit, and help him make more money. But you should also be using it for your own benefit, and for the benefit of your family.

Wouldn't it be nice if you could increase your own salary whenever you wanted to? If, whether you wanted to buy a new car, a new house, an expensive watch, or book a vacation for weeks in an exotic new location, you could simply snap your fingers and do it?

Wouldn't it be nice if you didn't have to beg your boss to open the money vault for you? If you weren't treated like a child asking for a raise in his allowance?

You can do it. You can gain the power and clout you need to raise your salary as often as you want.

Let me ask you some questions. Were you hired to make more or less money for your employer? Were you hired to increase or decrease production? Were you hired to expand or contract the number of products and services in your company's supply chain?

If you can help your boss create the company he wants, making more and more money, with greater and greater production, he will be happy to raise your salary, pay you commissions, give you paid time off, and even give you equity in his company. If you make him rich—and he knows he could not replace you—he will have no choice but to keep you happy.

Over the years, many people have written books about how to get a raise. Virtually all of them share the same tips: work harder, be on time, be a team player, go the extra mile for the company, etc. You can guess the rest. But none of these strategies empowers the employee in quite the same way as the information in this book.

Make no mistake: you deserve it. The Industrial Revolution scheme stole your right to riches and here's your opportunity to do something about it.

So how do you raise your own salary?

The concept is easy. You are an expert at what you do, and you bring value to people's lives with your expertise and execution, whether you clean shoes, work as a hotel receptionist, as a store manager, scrub houses, work security, sell gadgets, hand out fliers on the street, or check out groceries at the supermarket. If you are an employee and your employer has customers who pay him money, you can make money as an employeepreneur on top of the salary you are paid.

All you need to start earning more money is to make the decision to cut the umbilical cord that attaches you to your employer, and the outdated belief that the only way to make more money as an employee is by asking your employer for a raise. The same value that is available to your employer is available to you to create anything you want. Use that value to create within your employer's business platform. He has the resources you need.

But you do truly need to give yourself permission. We are brought up in a social system that kills our initiative. It cuts off our ambition to try for greatness. As children, our desires are crushed by authority figures who control our lives. As adults, we are still governed by those same authority figures and the social structure that forces us to ignore our own needs. We wait in line even when there's no one in front of us. There's never anyone in front of you. You don't compete with anyone for a salary raise—there's enough for you, if you can only see the truth.

This is your own destiny, your own life, and your own circumstances. The only thing standing in your way is your fear of getting what you want. Your Industrial Revolution mindset taught you that if you played by the rules, you could have anything you want—work hard, study hard, climb the ladder. Who said you have to climb and not jump? Who's running your life, the social herd mindset?

I want to give you an example of how employees in many industries don't understand the wealth they have around them. In 2011, I was acting as an English–Spanish interpreter for an American company and a Mexican company that traded in iron ore. Iron ore is a mineral from which iron can be extracted. There are many companies all over the world buying this mineral in one form or another, to make all kinds of products. The market is huge. But I want to bring your attention to the commission aspect of it.

During the course of my work as an interpreter, I learned that if you bring a customer to a mine and that customer signs a contract to buy a certain amount of iron ore, you get a commission every time the customer makes a purchase (the purchases are scheduled monthly). These are industrial purchases. We're talking hundreds of thousands of tons of iron ore.

It's not surprising to see commissions for brokers in the millions of dollars every month. So why are mines' employees not taking full advantage of the opportunities that lie right in front of them for the grasping?

It is because of the permission factor. Everyone limits their task to their job description and can't see beyond those duties. In a mine, there are many employees, executing a range of different functions, from the secretaries to the accountants, the manager, the cleaning crew, the security guards, the miners, the truck drivers, the port workers, or even the interpreter. All it takes is finding a new customer for the mine. The business wants new customers. They don't care who gets the commission. The opportunity is right there.

Can you see the power of giving yourself permission instead of waiting your turn? This is just one example—there are hundreds and hundreds of examples, from any industry. People are working for small salaries, but riches beyond their imagination surround them. These riches are available to them for the taking, not by the asking.

I always tell my clients that the planet is theirs and that there is enough for everyone. All they need to do to unlock the door to great abundance is create value for other people. Don't let society stamp a title on you. Every person has intrinsic value. You are born with the ability to create anything you want. Keep your eyes open and you can find the right opportunities everywhere in your employer's business or industry. But you have to stop behaving as society wants you to behave—as an employee with a limited vision and perspective.

Your title of employee doesn't mean that your brain should stop innovating and creating! If you live in a city and you take public transportation to work, I am sure you have seen the following scenario: you enter the train or bus and you see a lot of people sleeping until they get to their job, where they wake up and start functioning.

At the end of the day, they are already yawning again on the way home. When they get home, they eat, watch TV, and go right to sleep, to do the same thing again the next day. They are only active and awake when they need to be someone else's employee. They are never awake for themselves!

This is the employee mentality, but as an employeepreneur, your behavior must be different. You must retain an energy and zest for life in order to power your new ventures. Of course, this will be easier once you start working on developing ideas and projects. When you start seeing the real possibilities of raising your salary as high as you want, you will be as active as a bee as you search for and brainstorm new ways to bring customers to your employer's business, to better old processes, to innovate, and to create new products and services.

You can dramatically increase the amount of money you make in your job, but you need to activate your brain and learn as you go. It's a process—there's no right or wrong. Just get going. Before you know it, you will be collecting checks with larger and larger amounts of money.

Chapter 10
The Function of a
Business

Billions of people go to work each day, but most of them understand very little about the function of a business. Your employer's business is important to the community, city, and country in which it operates. To put this in perspective, do a little experiment or exercise. Close your eyes and imagine there are no businesses on the planet.

Imagine that each person would have to create every service and product in order to satisfy their own needs and wants—the bed where they sleep, the television they watch, the network of pipes to bring water to their house, their haircuts, manicures, the vehicles they use for travel (from cars to trains to airplanes), and on and on and on.

As you can see from this little thought experiment, the amount of value that the existence of business—including your employer's business—brings to people's lives is immeasurable. The function of business is to better the lives of people through services and products. A business is a living ecosystem. It's born, it grows, it multiplies, and it ends—just like the life of anything else in this world.

The key purpose of any business is growth—for the business owner, for the employees, and for its customers. In that sense, at any given point a business is either growing or it's dying. A business is growing when it is helping people to solve problems. The more people the business helps, the more money it makes for its owner and employees.

But businesses don't grow by default. They need all the help they can get from their owners, employees, and customers. Each plays a vital role in the development of the business. The owner provides the vision, money, and resources to get it going, the employees provide the force that moves the business forward each day, and the customers provide the much-needed cash flow to keep the business afloat.

Traditional mindsets can limit the power of all three key players. It can be a good idea to ask your employer to tell you his or her story. You are likely to hear a story of past financial struggles. You are likely to hear about long-held beliefs that can limit your employer's potential to grow the business.

Understand this: *you can help create a bigger company than the one you work for right now.*

But you are being limited by a job description that keeps the business from growing to its maximum potential. You can use the areas of the business that fall outside of your job description in order to make money for your employer and for yourself.

The customer's role is also limited when it comes to the growth of the business. How many times have you heard your boss or a co-worker—or even yourself—say to a customer, "We don't do that." Every time you hear that phrase, you need to ask yourself, "Why not?" Why can't your business do whatever it is the customer wants you to do? Hidden inside this question is the secret to your new ventures. It is the secret to making you rich.

Each time you hear a co-worker say those words, she is shutting down the business. When a customer asks a question—listen. When a customer complains—listen. A complaint is an opportunity. The customer is trying to make your employer's products or services satisfy a need or a want of which you are not yet aware.

Most business owners think that their job is done when they create their product or service. But that's just the start. The function of a business goes far beyond its physical structure, its products and services, or its employees' smiles and friendliness. Charles Revson (the founder of Revlon, one of the world's leading cosmetics companies) used to tell his employees, "In the factory, we make lipstick. In the store, we sell hope."

Your employer's offerings must transcend the utility of the products and services themselves. They must help customers do what all products and services must help people do: find hope, happiness, and life satisfaction.

A business exists to help expand the human experience. Maybe you've never heard a business defined this way, but think about it—when you want to buy a particular car and the price is more than you can afford, do you give up, or do you try to think of ways you can come up with the additional money and buy the car?

By extending yourself—by thinking beyond your present limitations and your lack of funds—you can reach for the unknown and further develop yourself.

You work more hours at work, thus creating more products and services for the benefit of your employer and for the benefit of the customer. You can also better the lives of other people by working smarter and becoming an employeepreneur.

Society advances each day because of the many problems all types of businesses solve. As an employeepreneur, you will need to focus completely on the problems your employer's customers are having. You need to find out the hopes and dreams that your company is failing to fulfill for its customers. And you need to find innovative ways to address those problems.

THE FUNCTION OF MONEY

When the Industrial Revolution took place, the role of money changed. It went from an object of consumption to an object of production. It became a psychological panacea capable of enhancing all aspects of life: family, food, entertainment, sex, and more. Money improves the lives of those who acquire it in great quantities.

Even though many people don't see it this way, I'm here to tell you that all of us are born into money. We are born into a global commercial economy that uses money as its basis of exchange.

Everyone is free to use it. But despite being surrounded by money in our daily lives, our personal feelings about money are often mixed. Money causes fear, love, desperation, expectation, hope—every emotion you can think of. Your feelings about money are a good indication of the amount of money you think you deserve.

Your belief system regarding money affects your relationship with it in every way. The biggest reason we feel anxious about money is that we have been taught that there's never enough of it. We hear this everywhere from the time we are young—in our homes, schools, churches, workplaces, on the street, etc.

If you believe what you hear, it will affect how much money you can make as an employeepreneur. If you approach money with fear and anxiety, you will suffer. But if you approach it with an open, relaxed mindset of abundance, you will always find new opportunities within your employer's company to make yourself more money.

Millions of people walk the planet with millions of dollars of excess money at their disposal. Whether it's a few dollars or tens of thousands, everyone has a certain amount of money they use for personal joy, satisfaction, and the pursuit of value. The only function of money is to be exchanged for value. Even when you give money away to charity or to a person on the street, you are still receiving value—you are receiving the feeling of generosity, the feeling of being able to make a difference in the world, and the feeling of knowing someone will get food on that day.

Money, when seen from this perspective, is detached from the belief that riches are limited and that there's not enough money for all of us to enjoy.

Most business owners see money as limited. They see it as something they must fight to strip out of the hands of as many customers as possible. What these businesses don't realize is that customers are more than willing to trade their money for products and services they perceive to be of high value.

Customers want to give their money to businesses because they want to get things that, to them, are more valuable than money. They want to enhance their lives!

WHAT YOU SELL

The minute you understand that you are not just selling shoes, financial services, books, perfume, educational materials, transportation services, or anything else, you will go from a mere seller of products and services to a seller of dreams, hopes, and happiness.

You're not actually selling a hammer—you're selling the hanging of a granddaughter's picture. You're not selling a vacuum cleaner—you're selling a clean house. You're not selling haircuts and cosmetics—you're selling the hope of finding a girlfriend or a husband.

The value you provide represents a benefit in the minds of the people to whom you present your products and services. People want to know what that benefit is. They will decide within a split second if they are interested or not.

Your customers and prospects don't care about your capabilities. They only want to know if you care about them and if you can help them solve their problems. That's the value they seek from your employer's company.

If you only present your capabilities ("me, me, me") to your potential customers, you'll be doing exactly what every other business does—allowing yourself to be lumped together with everyone else. As an employeepreneur, you have the resources already in place but you need to develop a strong positioning in the marketplace.

You need to be very clear about how you are perceived. Do you come across as caring? Are you friendly and approachable? The way your new personal brand communicates your message will say a lot about you—it will demonstrate your values, culture, and core beliefs. Before you sell any product or service, you are selling yourself. Make sure you are someone that a customer would want to buy.

Chapter 11
Presenting Your Ideas

In your employer's eyes, you are just another employee with a job description. You will need to change that perception as you continue on your way to becoming an employeepreneur. The way you present yourself and your projects must attempt to change that perception. Success in your new employeepreneur venture depends on it.

Whenever you come up with an idea you believe is worth pursuing, develop a presentation before you even mention it to your employer. Take the time necessary to do your homework to find out if the idea can stand on its own.

To develop effective presentations, you need to follow a simple process. You need to create presentations that present a project in a systematic way. You must show (1) the problem, (2) the solution, (3) the competition, (4) the marketing and sales, and (5) your all-star execution.

None of these steps should interfere with your boss's operations—they should in fact enhance the core business. Remember that your boss is investing valuable resources—she wants to see increases in sales in the shortest time possible. This is not her dream project—it is yours. Make it easy, with your unbelievably compelling presentations, for her to see the benefit of your idea on the spot.

Let's look at each component of the presentation more closely.

THE PROBLEM

Finding problems is not hard. We usually do it automatically. We look for defects in everything. When we meet someone, we look for a flaw. When we visit a home, we notice the crack in the wall. The normal course of action is to complain, but instead you need to see defects and problems for what they really are: *opportunities.*

Make sure that you understand all of the angles. How is the problem currently being addressed? What solutions are being implemented? What are the costs to the company in terms of time, money, and resources? How much could the company save or make if the problem magically disappeared? What would you need to do to make that happen?

Keep asking questions and make sure that you have the answers or at least an assumption. You will not always find all the answers you need, but the obvious ones should be a no-brainer to come by and make part of your presentation.

THE SOLUTION

If your boss knows about the problem, she has probably already thought about solutions. You need to anticipate the reasons why the obvious solutions aren't being applied. Are they too expensive? Can you find a way to implement them at a lower cost? Does the business not have enough resources? Are there innovations other people have created that your boss doesn't even know about? Can you bring new knowledge to the table that can help illuminate the answer?

Your solution should be easy to understand. When I create a logo for any of my projects, the first thing I do is show it to my kids. If they can't see the message right away, I know that I need to keep working until it is clear as daylight. Oversimplify the core ideas and then go deep into details, but first pull your audience into the presentation.

THE COMPETITION

You may come up with a product or service that has fierce competition in the marketplace, but that should not stop you. You can do it in a different way! Jack Dorsey and Noah Glass cofounded Obvious, a company aiming to provide podcast services (a podcast is a digital media broadcast consisting of video or audio streams).

When Apple launched iTunes, Dorsey and Glass realized that they couldn't compete. They started to look for ways to utilize their technology in a different way—and Twitter was born. New ideas can develop even when it seems like there is overwhelming competition!

MARKETING AND SALES

Make it easy for your boss or employer to understand your sales and marketing plan. You need to explain how you plan to introduce the product or service into the marketplace, or at least how the company should introduce it. Your employer may know the best way to introduce the product or service, but he surely wants to know if you did your homework.

YOUR EXECUTION

The execution plan needs to include every detail about what you need from your employer in terms of staff involvement, resources, and product and service quantities.

Your employer should want to know how you are portraying the company in the marketplace, what you are saying, and how you are saying it. Work with your employer to get on the same page—she has the right to control how her company is being presented.

A NOTE ABOUT DESIGN

Don't compromise. If you are not a skilled designer, hire one to create your presentations for you. In today's business world, design can sometimes play an even more important role than the product itself.

If you have a good product but it doesn't have good packaging, it's probably not going to sell. Design is communication. People are well informed about design ever since Apple revolutionized the presentation of products.

Every successful business on Earth is conscious of the power of design as a communicator of quality. There are many books and materials on how to create effective presentations. Here are some tools I find incredibly useful when it comes to creating my own presentations:

- *Killer Presentation Skills* (DVD, J. Douglas Jefferys)
- *The Perfect Pitch* (book, Jon Steel)
- *Microsoft PowerPoint* (presentation software)
- *Visual Thesaurus* (visual dictionary of synonymous)

These tools can turn you into an excellent presenter, provided that you practice, practice, practice.

Finally, if you want to put your employer at ease in the first five minutes of your presentation, offer complete risk reversal and a strong guarantee even before you start.

Risk reversal is the act of taking on or assuming all of the risk perceived in any business transaction. In business, and in life in general, we have been taught that for us to win, someone else has to lose. We approach all of our business negotiations with this mindset. But it doesn't have to be the case.

You can eliminate risk for your employer and make it easy for her to say yes to your plan. Explain that there is zero risk for the business, and offer a complete guarantee: "If I don't make X dollars by X date, you keep all the profit." Give your employer a bold and extreme guarantee.

Be willing to put it in writing. This type of guarantee will tell your employer that you are absolutely committed to the project and that you will bring revenue to the company, win or lose. This is a win-win proposition that an employer should not be able to resist.

Chapter 12
Your Personal Brand
Means Money

*When the voice and the vision on the inside become
more profound and more clear and loud than the
opinions on the outside, you have mastered your life.*
~John Demartini

Personal branding and social media (technology-
enabled word-of-mouth multiplied by millions of
voices using websites) have taken the marketplace by
storm. Today, there are individuals with larger fol-
lowings than billion-dollar corporations. People don't
want to follow companies—they want to follow actual
human beings. You can create a bigger following than
your employer's company can. All you need is to present yourself with authenticity, bring your own personality, and be real.

The main reason why people today (in the age of
social media) want to connect with other people is
that they want to experience something genuine and
real. Billions of people are waking up from decades
of branding and advertising by companies that didn't
care what their customers had to say. People no longer
want to hear lies and self-serving pitches.

Personal branding is so important today that many
companies are desperately looking for an edge when it
comes to reaching their intended audiences. In 2011,

will.i.am, music producer and front man for music group The Black Eyed Peas, was named Intel's Director of Creative Innovation.

This move by Intel, the popular computer chip maker, is a testament to the fact that personal branding is critical even for the largest companies.

If individuals are the new brands and the new faces of the corporations of the future, what does that mean for you as a new employeepreneur? It means that you can build your employeepreneur venture using your own personality and branding. The beauty of creating your own brand is that it can exist completely independently of your employer's business. Your personal brand is about you and can travel with you even when you leave your job.

Personal and business aspects of life are no longer as separated as they once were. People are integrating work into their lives in new ways. For many, there is no difference between what they do for work and what they do for fun. Work is becoming joyful, interesting, challenging, and rewarding.

Lawrence Pearsall Jacks perhaps said it best:

> The master in the art of living makes little distinction between his work and his play, his labor and his leisure, his mind and his body, his education and his recreation, his love and his religion. He hardly knows which is which. He simply pursues his vision of excellence at whatever he does, leaving others to decide whether he is working or playing. To him he is always doing both.

People around the world are searching for meaning in their jobs, personal lives, and relationships. Work is no longer only about money. It's also about finding meaning and enjoyment. People today do not last in jobs that are boring and lifeless. But for an employee-preneur, no job is boring! You create your own challenges—you create your own blend of business and pleasure, and you can find opportunities in any business setting.

Your personal brand is instrumental in helping you to achieve your professional goals. But you have to stand out from the crowd. There was a time when people feared showing their individuality. In some societies this may still be the case, but if you live in a modern, Western country, your own individuality can be your ticket to creating a remarkable personal brand.

You have personal traits, abilities, and characteristics that no other human being on the planet possesses. Find them, hone them, and show them off for the world to see. Creating your personal brand is like creating a brand new work of art.

Your personal brand must have a purpose: why are you doing whatever it is you do?

It must have a vision: where are you aiming to go?

It must have values: for what would you live or die?

Branding yourself as a unique and authentic person is the ultimate marketing tool of our time. The biggest names in the business world are realizing that personal branding is a major game-changer and, more and more, they are linking their personal brands to meaningful causes in order to boost their social standing.

If you have a strong brand, you have social value in the eyes of the world—and in the eyes of all of your potential customers. Your recommendations and opinions are valued and people listen to you. You become a trusted advisor and companies and individuals want to be around you and soak up your wisdom.

Your personal brand will help you immensely when it comes to increasing your salary, getting customers, getting referrals, and even expanding into new industries. Just like Dr. John Demartini has said, let your own voice and vision become your profound message.

Chapter 13
The New Consumer

I am sure you have heard the phrase, "The customer is always right," but have you heard the one that says, "The customer is in control"?

Well, the customer is indeed in control, and the sooner you come to terms with this, the sooner your employeepreneur venture will take off. You need to create a frictionless access platform for your customers: quick responses, respect for their time, easy access to products and services, and quick solutions. If you don't do these things and do them consistently, you will lose any customers you may find. Sometimes you will need to elevate your employer's typical standards of service in order to make your venture succeed, but anything you do to better your employer's business is to your benefit too! Remember that even if you have your employer's staff working on your behalf, you will be seen by your customers as the person to go to for anything that they might need. You are their first contact.

In the past, companies used to create their products and services without any input from consumers. Today, companies welcome and even seek out consumer input before they launch their products and services. The consumer has acquired tremendous power because the world has gone from mass production to mass consumption (savvy consumers and company transparency), and options to buy similar products and services have multiplied.

Why is it important for you to understand this from your new employeepreneur perspective? It is important because as an employee you may be exposed to only one aspect of servicing the customer, but as an employeepreneur your role will change from your limited job description to actually becoming a complete end-to-end manager for the customers you bring to your employer's business, depending on what you negotiate with your employer. You need to understand the entire customer experience because customers will come to you if anything goes wrong.

I want to compare yesterday's consumers with today's consumers so that you can see the differences and have a clear understanding of what you can expect from your customers and their behavior.

These comparisons will also help you find new ideas for products and services that will increase your salary. They will put into perspective what people all over the world are looking for and how they want to get it.

BARGAIN HUNTER VS. VALUE HUNTER

The old consumer was a bargain hunter. He wanted the lowest prices possible and didn't care much about value or benefits as long as he could satisfy his most pressing needs.

Today's consumer is different. She is a value hunter. She wants to find the best possible solutions and is ready to pay for them. She has many options to choose from and can't be bullied into buying anything she doesn't want. She will not be bullied by salesmen talking her to death until she finally submits. We now have the wisest and most informed consumers in the history of commercial business. They are pampered, they want to be served, and they want to be acknowledged and thanked as partners in the business.

As an employeepreneur, you need to keep in mind that the same challenges your employer has as a business will also face you in your ventures. You will not have concerns like health insurance for employees, business taxes, payroll, rent, etc., but you will face the very same challenges when it comes to finding, connecting, selling, and servicing customers. You could lose customers if you don't treat them well. You could get in trouble and damage your personal brand in the marketplace if you don't fulfill your promises and care for your customers. Just like any other business, you will be on display—because as an employeepreneur, you are the business.

WAIT FOR SOLUTIONS VS. FIND THEIR OWN

Yesterday's consumers waited for solutions from the companies they patronized. As an employee, many times you probably have heard a customer asking for new products or services or complaining about the existing ones. You may have found this behavior annoying and frustrating. However, as an employeepreneur you need to understand that the customer who complains is a customer who is waiting for your employer to come up with a solution to his problem.

Today's consumer finds another business to hand his money to—or, even better, creates the solution himself (and sometimes even starts his own business). Take the case of Netflix founder Reed Hastings. After returning from a vacation, he realized that he hadn't returned his Blockbuster DVDs and had to pay a $40 fine. He didn't like it, and went on to create an answer: Netflix. Today, Blockbuster is bankrupt and on the verge of disappearing, while Netflix thrives. The new consumer is not waiting. If your new venture can detect and respond quickly to these kinds of opportunities or problems, the sky is the limit.

TRUST ADVERTISING VS. DISTRUST ADVERTISING

If a company said something in its advertising, yesterday's consumer believed it. I am not implying that advertisers lie, but I am merely describing the beliefs of the past. Those were the days of mass production, when television and radio advertising were the only games in town. People were in awe of technology, and everything that came out of those devices was true, amazing, and fully believed.

Today's consumers don't believe in advertising. You say something and they want to verify it with others who have used your products and services. There is no trust in institutions. This is the main reason why personal brands today are becoming so powerful and important. Consumers want to have real people talking and selling to them. They don't want the fake smiles of the paid models on TV. They want authenticity. As an employeepreneur, if you can manage to be genuine and authentic, you will be successful with the new consumers.

TRUST PRODUCT INFORMATION VS. READ PRODUCT INFORMATION

Yesterday's consumers trusted the information displayed on products.

Today's consumers have lost trust in companies in all industries. Companies are supposed to be partners with consumers, because a sound and trusting relationship benefits both parties. But somewhere along the way, business owners, investors, and other executives in the business world got greedy and started abusing the company/consumer relationship. Today, if you turn over a product, most of them have customer service numbers for consumers to call and ask questions. In the past, this was unheard of.

Understand that as an employeepreneur, you should present yourself as a personal brand first, and once you have the necessary information to solve your potential customer's problems, then you present your offerings. People don't want to be sold—they want partners who understand them and want to help them first. It's not about you, and it's not personal. It's the reputation companies have created for themselves. You should act as a personal brand first.

FEW OPTIONS VS. TOO MANY OPTIONS

We are living in a connected world. Today, if you live in Germany and you want to buy a product in Brazil, all you have to do is go online, place the order, and choose your delivery preference. You get what you buy at the time you determine and in the way you determine. You can get anything you want in your local market just as easily as you can get it from the global marketplace.

In the past, the consumer was boxed in. He had the money, but the options were limited. Some businesses treated their customers badly because they could—there were no other options for the consumer. Now, the customer can sit at her desk, go online, and buy from anywhere in the world. If you don't have the right product, or don't have the time to help a customer, she will go somewhere else and may never come back.

DISCONNECTED VS. CONNECTED

Yesterday's consumer was isolated and disconnected. She couldn't verify the truth of an advertised product or service, or its performance, because the people around her—her neighbors—either didn't know about the product or knew of it but had never used it.

Today's consumer is connected to a global network of intelligent peers. This network is in operation 24/7 and 365 days a year. There are many governmental organizations that protect consumers, like consumerworld.org, or national organizations like the Better Business Bureau (in the United States: bbb.org).

Some of these companies protect consumers from fraud and provide information about laws and regulations. However, the best and most effective way consumers protect themselves is by reading reviews written by other consumers about businesses' products and services. These reviews come from what is known today as consumer-aggregated content. These are reviews that consumers write and post themselves on public websites like Yelp, Zagat, Facebook, Twitter, Trip Advisor, and many others. Consumers post comments about their experiences, good and bad, with particular companies. Trip Advisor, for example, is a consumer-aggregated content site for the hospitality industry (hotels, restaurants, spas, motels, etc.). This website has changed that industry forever. It has created remarkable improvements in the hospitality industry because hotels fear to death a bad comment. They know that if customers post bad comments or reviews about their hotels, others will stay away.

Businesses in the hospitality industry have upgraded everything from the infrastructure, products, and services to the ways they present their offerings to the public. All of these companies are adapting to the new reality of the marketplace: the customer is in control.

As an employeepreneur, you will be subject to scrutiny and reviews. They may not be at the level of a big company or organization, but rest assured that people you don't know will hear about the products and services you offer—and they will make their decision about whether or not to buy.

Chapter 14
Creating Products and Services

Regardless of the type of business your employer owns, there are two areas you need to watch like a hawk and keep in mind when looking to develop new products, services, or innovations: (1) revenue increase—where he spends money to create new business opportunities, and (2) business overhead—where he spends money to maintain the business operations.

If you pay attention to these two areas in your employer's business, you will find golden opportunities to make or save money for your boss.

Any new service, product, or innovation will have a direct impact on the business in one or both of these areas. You will either make more money for your employer or save him money that he is currently spending. Increases in revenue and decreases in overhead spending are always welcomed, in any business.

Increasing revenue (more customers, products and services, and innovations) tends to offer a wider range of opportunities because this area is not constrained by the services and products your employer must use in the business to keep it running smoothly.

In terms of revenue increase, the sky is the limit. Your employer will never be able to capture and control the entire universe of opportunities and resources to grow his business. This is your greatest opportunity to make money for you and for him.

But let's talk first about business overhead—where he spends money to maintain the business. Saving money implies that a product or service is being bought at a particular price, and that a better price might exist. Finding this cheaper option for the same product or service is a critical way for you to make an impact.

Take this letter as an example:

Mr. Boss,

I know you are buying flour for the bread we make here at 5 cents above the market price, because the supply we get is consistent and reliable. What if I could help you save 7 cents per pound, while exceeding the reliability and consistency of the current supplier, guaranteeing the price for a set time in the contract, and instead of you having to pick up the flour and spending time and money on gas, it would be delivered to us here at the door?

You would save hundreds of thousands of dollars every year. Now, what percentage of the savings would you give to the person who could bring this new supplier to you?

Sincerely,
Your Employee

Does it sound impossible? These kinds of deals happen every day all around the world. Just make sure that you have already declared your position as an employeepreneur before you start this kind of conversation, because you don't want to seem ungrateful and even disloyal to your boss. After all, he's doing you a favor by giving you a job—*he may very well think that you should be grateful and loyal and bring to him all opportunities that can help the company, without expecting any compensation in return.* Most employers don't see (or prefer not to see) the value employees bring to their companies. For them, employees are expenses instead of investments. Prove them wrong by making more money than your immediate boss.

This is just a tiny example of finding an area inside your employer's business where he can save money. You can apply this concept to the electric bill, taxes, accounting services, cleaning services, food and beverage supplies, marketing and advertising expenses, and so much more. Find the areas where money is being spent, and, yes, help your boss save money—but don't neglect to ensure you are compensated for your efforts.

Let's now look at revenue increases—where money is being spent to create new business opportunities. Getting new customers, creating new products and services, and bringing innovation into a business are not just the domains of management—they are up for grabs. You, right now, as an employee, can get a multi-million-dollar customer for your employer at any time or create a star product or service.

Anything that can increase the bottom line of your employer's company is open to you; you have access to it because it is under the control of no one.

For example:

Ms. Employer,

I was on a vacation with my family in Singapore last week and met John Smith. John has a unique business in which he uses melted plastic to create unique shapes by throwing the plastic in an icy fluid very similar to the fluid we produce here in our factory.

I inquired about John's business and discovered that the icy fluid solution he is using is not cost-effective and the results are not ideal. Our product can perform better. There's only one modification we would need to make, and he even offered to cover the cost of that modification if we were willing to start testing within the year.

John is ready to buy half a ton of our icy fluid solution every month if our product proves to be more cost-effective than what he's currently using, with equivalent or better results.

What percentage of this new business revenue would you give to the person who could bring this new customer to you?

Sincerely,
Your Employee

The question is in the third person, because if you just started your employeepreneur venture, Ms. Employer will see you as an employee and have a hard time admitting that you deserve a substantial amount of money. Be flexible but also understand the hundreds of thousands—or even millions—of dollars in extra revenue that you will be bringing to her company.

This is your strongest negotiating point: you will bring her "free" customers on whom she will not have to spend any money because you will use your own money to travel, market, event network, or attend conferences. This gives you the power to earn a larger share of the profits—a very different situation than if you were *only* an employee getting paid a fixed salary for everything you do.

You can create all kinds of projects, non-stop, day and night, using your imagination, ingenuity, and creativity. If you turn your job into a testing lab, and integrate the steps explained throughout this book into solving problems for your employer, you will live a life you could have never imagined.

Here's how to find solutions to problems and develop products and services in four easy steps:

1. Identify the problem,
2. Gather information,
3. Filter the information,
4. Develop your product or service.

IDENTIFY THE PROBLEM

People complain about problems, but very few try to find solutions. Finding solutions to problems that make life easier for everyone is big business—and you have all you need to do it right where you work.

Products fail or become inefficient, services fall short of their promises, and processes need updating. These shortcomings cause problems for companies. A problem is usually a hindrance to progress. All businesses all over the world have problems and they pay big money to anyone who solves those problems for them.

These three easy steps will help you identify problems in your company.

1. Follow the pain

A problem causes pain. By "follow the pain" I mean listen to the complaints from your employer, coworkers, and customers and you will find the main cause of the problem affecting them.

2. Check for accepted consequences

Another way to identify problems is by checking for consequences. The effects of many problems are accepted and never questioned because no one has ever found a solution, or just because that's how things have been for a long time. Find those silent and culturally accepted consequences to problems that no one complains about; they hold the biggest rewards. This requires analytical thinking and a high level of attention, but it's doable.

3. Update your knowledge of laws and regulations

Laws and regulations also represent problems and limitations to business developments. Your employer can't keep up with everything related to his business. It's impossible. He may have certain control inside the business, but what happens outside the business is another story.

Find out about laws and regulations that impact your employer's business and see if you can find ways to go around them without violating those laws. Ideas and innovations that couldn't be implemented in the past might get a green light with the passage of new laws.

When you encounter a problem of any kind, don't complain. Look at it as a puzzle that needs an answer. Get out of the reaction mode that most business owners, employees, and people in general live in. Open your mind. Try to see the world in another way.

GATHER INFORMATION

Once you identify a problem, get as much information as you can. Our subconscious mind is incredibly skilled at solving problems when we know what the problem is and feed it the necessary information. So gathering information to solve a particular problem is the second step, after we have identified the problem that we want to solve.

There are two kinds of information: general and specific. When gathering information to solve a particular problem, it's always a good idea to start with a general information perspective and then move on to gather as much specific information as possible about the particular problem. General information includes everything from looking at different business models, to reading a wide range of topics to try to see other people's points of view, to trying to create relationships with the specific problem. This will open up new possibilities (and even markets) for the solutions you're trying to come up with, because one solution may have many applications.

Specific information includes anything that's directly related to the specific problem you have identified. There are many places and sources you can use to get specific information; however, when sourcing information for a particular problem, the first place to start is with real people. People have the raw information because they are the ones affected by the problem and can give you personal, first-hand accounts of the consequences of a problem. They will give you factual and relevant information that will put you on the right track, if you succeed in asking the right questions.

Conduct interviews. Start with emotional questions: how does it feel not to be able to...? When do you need it most? How does it affect your life or the lives of your loved ones? How are you dealing with it without having the right solution?

Keep digging deeper with follow-up questions on the answers they give you. Author Karen Cushman said it best: "I think sometimes that people are like onions. On the outside smooth and whole and simple but inside ring upon ring, complex and deep." Dig deeper if you want to find the gold. You will not find it on the surface. Follow all of the words that suggest pain, frustration, or the contrary: hope and happiness.

In essence, when you research general and specific information with a particular outcome in mind, you are cross-pollinating or influencing different elements to bring them together and create new ones. This may seem chaotic to our conscious mind, but your subconscious mind thrives in this type of environment because it can reference and make millions of connections with the information that we feed it. As ad executive James Webb Young said, "The capacity to bring old elements into new combinations depends largely on the ability to see relationships."

FILTER THE INFORMATION

Even though your subconscious mind can work miracles, ultimately you need to filter the information it gives you with your conscious mind and make some sense of it. Filtering all of this information involves taking what's relevant and leaving behind what is not relevant. However, don't discard anything just yet.

What I mean is that you should write down everything that comes to mind related (or not) to the topic. Carry a small notepad or an electronic device to record any idea that you think of, regardless of how crazy it sounds. Before you go to sleep, let your mind run wild imagining that the product or service you want to bring to market is already out there and you are merely trying to grab it.

This type of imagery will push your subconscious mind to make even more connections. Have a pad and pen by your bed in case any idea comes to mind in the middle of the night.

Albert Einstein once said, "The true sign of intelligence is not knowledge, but imagination." Imagination is how we make impossible connections, dream incredible dreams, and accomplish impossible feats. Imagination is what takes us beyond our present situation to places where we can visualize solutions and come back victorious. The more you play with the information—writing, visualizing, charting, and talking about it to trustworthy people— the more your mind will understand what you are looking for.

In his classic book *Psycho Cybernetics*, Dr. Maxwell Maltz talks about the theater of the mind. His book is an amazing resource about the power of the subconscious mind. I recommend it highly. The theater of the mind is the act of seeing with your imagination the outcome of what you desire—seeing it as if it is already a reality. To practice this technique, he advises the reader to relax his body by lying down and letting his mind create the outcome he desires. Since your subconscious mind can't tell reality from illusion, it can start to believe that what is being reflected is real, and then try to recreate those exact images in the physical world using the conscious mind.

DEVELOP YOUR PRODUCT OR SERVICE

If you already have an idea of the product, service, innovation, or process improvement that you want to create for your employer, then it's time to turn it into something real and tangible—give it form, function, and utility.

In Chapter 10, we discussed your presentations. Here I would like to talk about a related topic—forming the products, services, innovations, or process improvements that you want to create for the benefit of your employer and yourself.

After you have determined that it is worth pursuing the idea or project, you need to shape it with the input of other people. The sooner you get this input, the faster you will move in the process. Remember that you don't have all the answers. If your idea is for a tangible product, you can now easily create a mock-up using 3D technology. Never talk about something if you can show it, and never merely show it if you can demonstrate it. So, if possible, create a sample.

It causes a more powerful effect if you can put it on the presentation table. Let your boss touch and admire the prototype. Show its functionality and benefits. Today, there are many companies that provide 3D printing services: Shapeways.com and Object.com are just two examples. They specialize in 3D printing or rapid prototyping. This new concept is revolutionizing manufacturing and product distribution on a global scale because these companies are not only printing prototypes in 3D—they are also using a Print-On-Demand business model (printing or manufacturing the product only after a customer has purchased it).

If your idea or project is for services or process improvements, then presenting the complete solution as graphically as possible is the best approach. Make sure that you received feedback from people with experience in the topic. There are many ways that pictures and graphics can tell a complete story; use them. We are bombarded by too much written and oral information. Pictures speak louder than words.

Chapter 15
Marketing for
Employeepreneurs

Peter Drucker is one of the most widely known thinkers and writers on the subject of business management. One of his most famous quotes is the basis of what can become your strongest advantage in your pursuit of making money using your employer's resources.

Drucker said, "Business has only two functions: marketing and innovation."

Every business needs customers and constant innovation. If you can provide either of these to your employer, he will be happy to share the increased profits with you. If you don't work directly in customer acquisition, then this could be an amazing opportunity for you to bring new customers to your employer. If customer acquisition is not one of your job duties, then there would be no confusion here—if you bring the customer in, credit belongs to you. Any employee can innovate for their employer in terms of new products and services, processes improvements, etc., and get the rewards from their efforts. To do this, you need to become a double agent—a spy. You need to perform the duties of an employee and the secret duties of an employeepreneur. Your duties as an employee are the ones you were hired to do; your duties as an employeepreneur are the ones you will create yourself: marketing, research, projects, presentations, and idea development.

One of your challenges will be making a clear distinction between your job duties and the new revenue you are bringing into the business. If, for instance, you sell shoes, it would be hard to prove to your employer that you marketed and brought a new person in from the street to buy shoes—but if you contact a company or organization and put them in direct contact with your boss or employer, that can prove that you made the initial contact with that particular customer.

Simply stated, marketing is any activity a company does to attract and retain customers. Marketing is composed of three factors: (1) the message, (2) the audience, and (3) the media.

THE MESSAGE

Every employeepreneur needs to create his or her own Unique Selling Proposition (USP). A USP is a simplified statement of the solutions and benefits you can offer in the marketplace. It tells prospective customers why they should buy from you instead of your employer's competitors. It is critical—customers want to know how you can help them, if they can trust you, and if you have what it takes to help them solve their problems.

Your USP must convey a strong message about the essence of your employer's business—a concise description of the offerings, the quality, the guarantees, and the benefits. And just as you reverse the risk of your new ventures from your employer to you, you should also reverse the risk of doing business with your employer's company from your potential customers to you and your employer. They should genuinely have nothing to fear or lose.

I want to share an example of one business that used its USP to grow from obscurity into one of the biggest brands in the world today. In 1960, Tom Monaghan and his brother James purchased a failing pizza restaurant named Dominick's, located near Eastern Michigan University. Eight months later, James traded his half of the business to Tom for a used Volkswagen Beetle because he saw no future in the company. In 1965, as sole owner of the business, Tom renamed it Domino's Pizza, Inc. In 1967, the first Domino's Pizza franchise location opened in Ypsilanti, Michigan.

The rest is history. But I want to bring to your attention how it happened for Tom and for Domino's. The USP that changed the fate of that unsuccessful pizza place was this: fresh, hot pizza, delivered in thirty minutes—or it's free. This USP was successful because it was short, to the point, and contained a declaration of confidence, benefits, and commitment to the customer.

Most importantly, it provided a powerful call to action. Everyone wants fresh food, fast. By giving a definite timeframe, and providing a guarantee, the customer's risk was eliminated from the transaction. That elimination of risk, combined with the promise of a fresh, delicious product, caused customers to rush to place their orders.

The right USP can provide awesome power to your employeepreneur venture. Following are some USPs that make customers stop and pay attention.

Palmolive: "Softens hands while you do dishes."

FedEx: "When it absolutely, positively has to be there overnight."

Dalton McCrary's How to Hit the Golf Ball as Straight as You Can Point: "I teach people how to hit a golf ball as straight as they can point, or the lesson is free...and I'll give them twenty-five dollars for wasting their time."

The third example is the strongest. If these three businesses were offering the same product, I would buy from Dalton McCrary, and I have a feeling that you would too. Make your USP strong and, above all, make sure it provides a genuine benefit for your customers and your prospective customers. Your USP should answer the question that's always in the minds of prospective customers: "With so many options in the marketplace, why should I choose your business over all the rest?" You need to answer this question in a split second. They need to know the reason why. If you can't answer that question, how can you expect your customers to?

Coming up with just the right USP isn't easy. It's hard, because you have to dig deep to find the essence of what your employer's company represents in the marketplace, and then dig even deeper to express it in as few words as possible.

You're not merely creating a mission statement that tells the world about your aspirations, how great the company is, and how long it's been in business. You have to give them more—with less.

How do you come up with the perfect USP? Follow the steps below.

Step 1: Find the business essence

Before you start writing the USP, you need to start looking for guidance in two places: the business and the customers.

The business

Write a questionnaire about the business. Probe deeply for insights into the benefits the company offers. Why do we exist? Who are we? What benefits do we bring to the marketplace? How do we transform people's lives for the better?

Don't stop until you have at least fifty questions. Yes, fifty! Ask the same question from different angles. Why do our benefits help customers? How do they help men/women/children? Look at the business like an outsider. And don't stop asking questions until you have a rich understanding of why the company exists and what unique value it brings to the market.

The customers

When you are talking to customers, ask them questions about the business. They will be happy to talk to you. People love giving input to businesses they patronize. Ask open-ended questions to capture as much information as possible. Probe deeply for insight into how the business is perceived by outsiders.

For instance: You've been our customer for a long time. Why? What do you like about our services? What are some of the benefits we provide that make your life easier? What problems do we solve? What would you add to our offerings? This last question is so simple and yet so powerful. I compare it to the simple question McDonald's asks its customers: "Would you like fries with that?"

This simple question has increased revenue for the restaurant franchise by millions upon millions of dollars. You will find valuable information that will lead to a solid USP (and even ideas to make money with your employer's resources). If you have repeat customers, it's because you are providing real value. Find out what that value is and integrate it into your USP.

Step 2: Identify the main problems you solve

Step 1 provided information about the benefits you provide and the problems you are solving for your customers. But the easy answers aren't enough. Keep digging for more, and don't stop until you've identified at least twenty-five to fifty problems that you are solving for people. This exercise will give you great insight into your company and further sharpen your USP.

Step 3: Start matching the biggest problems with the most critical solutions.

Match the biggest problems with the biggest solutions you offer. This will give you the clearest picture of the value your company brings to the marketplace. But you must go beyond the surface. You need to look for the real, intimate value that customers are getting from their experiences. In this step, you start to connect the dots and clarify what is really the key driver of sales—and what makes the company special and valued.

Step 4: Your guarantees and promises

If your customers keep coming back for more, it's because the business is working and you are delivering quality products and services.

Now, verbalize and write the promise or guarantee into your USP, and you will be closer to magic than you think. Make your guarantee a jaw-dropping move. Your guarantee should motivate people to take action. Depending on your negotiations and level of trust with your employer, you know how far you can go with your promises and guarantees.

Step 5: Take the biggest benefits, promises, and guarantees—and start writing possible USPs

Write at least twenty USPs. Don't think too hard or analyze them too much. Just write them down as they come to mind. Your subconscious will create new connections and bring ideas forth as you write. Don't question anything—just write. Stay as close to Dalton McCrary's example as you can, in terms of length—or go even shorter: "I teach people how to hit a golf ball as straight as they can point, or the lesson's free, and I give them twenty-five dollars for wasting their time."

Step 6: Combine and rewrite

Get someone (a team member, customer, or marketing expert) to help you choose the USPs that best reflect the products, services, and culture of the company you work for. Find words in your USPs that are meaningful and stand on their own. Underline or highlight them. After you have selected the best, combine them all into the best three sample USPs you can create. Then combine them again and rewrite until you get to the one perfect USP that you can use for your marketing campaign. If you created others that are also great, don't discard them—you can use them for other marketing material in the future.

This is a long process that requires time and dedication. Some business owners work at creating their USPs for months, if not years. Start the process now to create this amazing marketing tool and you'll be delighted with how people respond.

You might be thinking, why do I need another marketing message if I will use my employer's business? The short answer is that, as an employeepreneur, you are an independent agent. The same way that you will sell your innovations to your employer and to your new customers, you can sell them to other businesses in the same or different industry. Think about it. Why limit yourself?

You will be using your employer's infrastructure, not his marketing message and his media; if you did that, you would fall back into an employee role. You need to keep things separate. Remember, you need to keep three things separate from the very beginning: (1) your job as an employee must be separate from your venture as an employeepreneur (agent), (2) your marketing and innovation methods must be different from your duties as an employee, and (3) your employeepreneur venture brand should be connected directly to you. As an employeepreneur, you are a free agent, you are your own brand.

THE AUDIENCE

You didn't have a choice as far as the family you were born into, the body you were born with, or the place of your birth. But if you're going to become an employeepreneur, you have a choice as far as the customers you want to work with. As an employee, you have to serve any customer who comes to your employer's business, but as an employeepreneur, you have the power to choose.

The act of choosing your customers is as important as crafting your marketing message (USP). You can't expect great results and effective marketing campaigns if you don't know who your customers are or how to find them. I'm confident that while crafting your USP, you had glimpses into who your ideal customers are, or at least who you want them to be.

Crafting your message should have clarified some important aspects about the people you consider your ideal customers—you must pay attention to their age, gender, marital status, location, lifestyle, income level, occupation, and more. When you've defined your market, it's a lot easier to identify your targets in a crowd. This may seem like common sense, but common sense is not always common practice. You would be shocked to know how many business owners think every single person out there is a target customer.

As an employeepreneur, your time is limited. You have a full-time or part-time job, family, and may have other obligations. The potential customers you choose to go after have to be worth your time and effort. Once you know your target market, you have an advantage that few other business owners have—and you can seek out the kinds of places you know your audience will gravitate toward.

Today, you can purchase customer lists based upon any of the characteristics I mentioned: age, gender, income level, location by zip code, education level, marital status, ethnicity, etc. Although the best customer list is one you create yourself, buying a list from a list broker can give you a head start. To find list brokers, you can conduct a search in your local library in the database SRDS: Standard Rate and Data Service. Or you can buy the yearly membership at their website. This database contains information about media rates (advertising prices). It lists circulation and other basic information for a broad range of media outlets that sell advertising space. The SRDS contains demographic and market information for metropolitan areas and counties in the United States, Canada, and 200 other countries. It also has over 70,000 consumer lists and provides the contact information for the brokers that represent those lists.

Below are the demographic characteristics you need to understand in order to define and identify your target audience. Narrowing things down will help you identify new customers for your employer's products and services.

Gender

If your employer caters to women only, just as an example, you might want to try to find a way to adapt the product or service to men. We all know that the beauty business caters primarily to women. But men are becoming more and more interested in their personal image. If your employer doesn't serve men, you can create new products and services that would attract them. This would open up entirely new market opportunities for your employer and for you.

Age

You need to know the age group of the target audience you're going after. The age of your prospective customers determines where you will look for them.

If your employer's customers typically range between 25 and 35 years old, you could open new markets in the 15-to-20-year-old range by adapting the products and services or creating new lines.

Location

If your employer's offerings can be delivered anywhere in the world, you would have a global marketplace to experiment with your ideas and this would open up amazing opportunities to increase your salary.

But even if your employer's business is local and there's no way to make it a global business, you can still innovate within the company or create new products and services that could be sold on a global scale.

Income level

Income is important because you want to make sure that the customers you attract can actually pay for the products and services you sell without asking for discounts or complaining about your prices. A person making $20,000 a year will not be looking for the same services as someone making $120,000 a year. Individual consumption levels and available income to spend will be very different.

Education level

Education is important. Today, many people join networking groups of similarly educated individuals—lawyers, doctors, college alumni groups, etc. You can join particular groups on websites like LinkedIn, Eventme, Eventbrite, and many others. These can start to introduce you to the right targets.

Occupation

What your customers and potential customers do for a living is important. Depending on the kind of company you work for, it might be easy for you to find customers according to their profession. Here, again, networking groups can come in handy. Professionals and business owners in different industries meet frequently in different cities around the world. This makes it easy for you to find and pitch them.

THE MEDIA

Many people in business jump directly to media, which should be the last step. This happens because a lot of people don't understand that the media is only a vehicle and nothing more.

After you have created your marketing message and identified your target audience, you can proceed with the final step of deciding what vehicles you will use to bring your message to your target market.

Your first and most obvious option is mass media: television, radio, the Internet, books, magazines, newspapers, billboards, signs, skywriting, blimps, advertising on buses or taxis, milk cartons, and countless other places. Mass media advertising, although expensive, is the best way to advertise when everybody is your customer.

But if you've selected a narrow market segment and you know enough about them, you can reach them exclusively by using targeted media communication like direct mail marketing, email marketing, door to door solicitation, fax broadcasts, or possibly telemarketing.

Chapter 16
Direct Marketing

Direct marketing is the targeting of pre-selected customers or prospects. This pre-selection is (or should be) based on information regarding products or services that people have shown interest in by participating in a survey, joining a mailing list, subscribing to a magazine, or requesting more information about a particular product or service. Some of the communication channels used in direct marketing include telemarketing, fliers, postcards, text messaging, email marketing, direct mail marketing, networking, and social media. (Note that telemarketing doesn't work for direct sales in the USA anymore. Many people are on the National Do Not Call Registry and calling them can get your business in trouble. However, if you want to conduct a survey, you can call anyone, as long as you don't try to sell them anything.)

EMAIL MARKETING

Email marketing is the electronic version of direct mail marketing. To send commercial emails to potential customers, you need their permission. If you send them emails without their permission, it is considered spam and there are many email providers that send these kinds of emails directly to the trash or spam bin.

You can get email addresses online or offline from potential customers who show interest in your employer's products and services. To get email addresses online you can use a web form where the prospect enters their name and email address. There are many other methods you can use to get email addresses. For example, if you have a website, you can offer contests, reports, webinars, or any other type of benefit that would make your prospects want to give you their email addresses.

Since you can't approach your employer's customers to ask them for their email addresses, getting email addresses offline can be a little more difficult. But depending on your company and industry, you could be in a position to take advantage of opportunities that other people in other industries and companies wish they had. If you're considering email marketing, these are some tools that can prove helpful. There are many more resources online, but these should get you started.

Domain name

A domain name is like your home address. This is the electronic address people will type in the Internet browser to find your website. If possible, buy a domain name with the ending .com. This means that your website is for commercial purposes. This is the most recognized format for domain names on the Internet.

Some good companies to buy a domain from are 1and1.com, namecheap.com, and godaddy.com. Go to their websites and learn all you can about their prices and services.

Hosting company

A hosting company is the place where your website and all its documents, links, pictures, reports, etc. will be located. Think of this as a storage place for websites.

There are some good and cheap companies out there: hostgator.com and bluehost.com are two nice ones. Check them out and make your own decision.

WordPress.org

This is a free open-source platform (free and open to developers who want to better the platform) where you can create websites. Most of the blogs and websites you see today are created on this platform. It's easy to use and very powerful.

Aweber or Mail Chimp

These two companies offer services for email marketing. Every time a new person subscribes to your email list, these companies' software sends the person an automated message welcoming them and letting them know what your company is about. You create and set these messages in a systematic way so that your list receives your messages in the order you organize it. Check these two companies out and choose the one that can best help you with your goals.

D<small>IRECT MAIL MARKETING</small> (<small>SALES LETTERS</small>)

Copywriting is the art of writing content for advertising that sells your employer's products and services.

It is a profession, just like graphic design or architecture. It would be impossible to teach you copywriting within the limited space of this book. However, I will give you some pointers using direct mail marketing that will guide you in beginning to create effective sales letters to market your employer's products and services. Keep in mind that these copywriting techniques can be used with any other direct marketing channel you decide to use.

You can write a sales letter for the products and services you sell—and do a better job than many professional consultants—because no one understands your employer's offerings as well as you do. You possess the knowledge that only experience can provide, but you do need to practice the art of copywriting. This is an art not practiced very well in most mainstream businesses. Most likely, your employer doesn't use direct mail sales letters. He should—but if he doesn't, you have an even bigger advantage.

The best way to learn copywriting in a matter of weeks is by rewriting sales letters from the masters, by hand. No computers—use pen and paper. Use your favorite search engine (Google, Yahoo, Bing, etc.) to find sales letters from master copywriters like Jay Abraham, Dan Kennedy, and Gary Halbert. Gary's letters, for instance, are at thegaryhalbertletter.com and are all free to read or print.

These are three of the best copywriters I know and from whom I have learned. Read about them. Rewrite their letters and soon you will be writing amazing sales letters just like them. You can also join their mailing lists to receive their regular updates.

When considering a direct mail campaign using sales letters, every element is important. However, there's a certain order that needs to be followed. You need to guide your customers and prospective customers to do exactly what you want them to do and to see the unique benefits of the products and services you sell.

For your sales letter to be effective, it needs to contain the following elements below.

1. A pre-selected audience (customers or prospects)
2. The envelope (packaging)
3. The headline (attention grabber)
4. The sub-headings (secondary attention grabber)
5. The ad copy (designed to elicit strong emotions)
6. Testimonials (great things your customers say)
7. The guarantee (100% full refund)
8. Supply limitation (only 20 items left)
9. Time sensitivity (two days only!)
10. The call to action (order now before we run out)
11. How to order
12. Your contact information

A pre-selected audience

A pre-selected audience is the most important element in any direct mailing campaign. Here the SRDS database can come in handy. You can define the customers you want, call a broker, and get exactly what you need.

Selling to a pre-selected audience will give you more bang for your buck, fewer wasted resources, a better chance for your campaign to be successful, knowledge about what your customers are buying and not buying, and the convenience and power of familiarity, which happens when customers know you and like what you offer them.

The envelope

Consider the envelope as the door that needs to be opened. People usually read their mail next to their wastebaskets. If the envelope isn't official (taxes, government communication, legal notices) or obviously personal (postcards, invitations, greeting cards) and it doesn't grab their interest in a split second, it may go straight into the trash, unopened.

You can have the best offer in the world, but if your letter isn't opened and read, it won't matter. Handwrite the prospect's name and address on the envelopes. If your handwriting is like mine, I recommend that you find someone with beautiful handwriting to write them for you instead. Avoid cursive; use only nice print handwriting.

This instantly adds a personal, human touch, which is especially rare in this day and age. People will feel more inclined to open your letter, which is the first and most important step in any direct mailing campaign, if they see that the letter was sent by a person and not a company.

The headline

This is the attention grabber. If you confuse the reader here, you've lost them forever. When you read something that you have to think hard about, to determine exactly what the message is, do you continue reading it or do you toss it in the garbage?

A benefit-loaded headline will make your potential customers raise their hands, especially if your offer is personal to them, based on their interests, likes, age, and lifestyle. It should be strong and to the point, with a big payoff that makes the reader stop and pay attention. Your headline should pique their interest so they continue reading.

In essence, a great headline gives you the opportunity to get your customers' attention and the ability to identify your audience in a split second. It eliminates time-wasting leads (a lead is an initial contact with a potential customer) and motivates your prospective customers to read the whole letter in order to find out how to get your offer.

The sub-headings

In the sub-headings, you'll ask questions that relate to the benefits in the headline. These questions will probe for the pain the customer is experiencing due to not having your product or service.

Probing for pain can also be an effective way to open in the headline. Believe it or not, some people will read your headline, sub-headings, and guarantees, and then go straight to the order section. These are people who have been waiting for someone like you to come to them with a solution to one of their biggest problems.

In essence, great sub-headings give you a chance to ask key questions, a chance to give your prospect a picture of the whole offer, the opportunity to address the pain that their problem is causing them, the opportunity to draw readers into your letter, and the chance to force your readers to further examine themselves.

The ad copy

Consider the copy or body of the letter to be your sales force in action. The ad copy has to tell a complete story of what you are selling and why. Tell your prospective customers everything about your products and services. People read when they are interested. That's why a pre-selected audience is paramount to succeeding in direct mailing.

Be sure to write about all of the benefits associated with the offer—every single one. People like benefits. Put yourself in the shoes of the reader. Everyone wants to know how a product or service can enhance their lives, make them more beautiful, more intelligent, faster, richer, etc.

In essence, the ad copy or offer gives you the chance to explain in detail what you sell, the chance to tell stories related to your offer, and the opportunity for the reader to learn more about you and your business.

The testimonials

Why are testimonials important? Here's an example. Suppose you're shopping in a mall and you happen to meet a friend. You start a conversation and the subject of lower back pain comes up. Standing near you is a man who happens to be a chiropractor. The man is close enough to hear your conversation. At the first opportunity, he comes over and introduces himself to tell you what a wonderful chiropractor he is. He tells you he's an expert at relieving back pain and that he has helped thousands of people with their back problems.

What would be your first reaction? To run away, I imagine. But let's suppose instead that your friend tells you about this wonderful chiropractor who cured her husband's back pain. Would you ask her for his name and number? I bet you would. This is evidence of the power of personal testimonials and recommendations. Third-party validation is the most effective tool you can use to introduce your products and services, because you can break the trust barrier almost instantly.

Direct mail marketing is about building trust and putting your target audience at ease as fast as possible. In essence, including a great testimonial gives you the advantage of a third-party validation, the ultimate tool to create trust (an endorsement), and the opportunity to show your prospective customers that what you say about your business is true and that your products and services really work.

The guarantee

The transfer of risk from your prospective customer to you is the most powerful tool you can use today when selling by direct mail. When you're presenting your offer to prospective customers who have never done business with you, you're asking them to take a huge risk. Always offer a strong guarantee to calm their fears.

Example: "If you are not completely satisfied with this product, please return it within 30 days for a full refund. I am 100% certain that you will be happy with our product. That is why I make this guarantee." Your employer would need to be onboard for you to make this offer, but if she believes in her products and services, I don't think it would be a problem.

Offering a guarantee gives you the chance to transfer all of the risk from your target audience to yourself. This clears the way for them to take action and buy from you. It gives you the chance to put your prospective customers at ease and to tell them that you are trustworthy.

Supply limitation

Using the concept of supply and demand is key when it comes to direct mail marketing. You have to make the reader believe that the offer is limited and that she has to take action now or she might lose the opportunity to get the deal you are offering her.

For instance, if you have a list with two hundred customers, you want your offer to make it seem as if not everyone will be able to have it. "We only have sixty remaining—hurry!"

A supply limitation gives you the perception of higher value, motivates your customers to buy more quickly, and instills the fear that if they don't act quickly, they'll miss out on a great opportunity.

Time sensitivity

A time-sensitive offer works much the same way as an offer with limited supply. But in this case it's a limit on time, not supply. Putting time-sensitive offers in your sales letter is ideal when you have recurring products, services, or packages to sell, such as with a monthly or yearly customer membership program.

A time-sensitive offer gives you control over the timeframe of the order process, momentum for the next round of sales, and lets you capitalize on the customer's urge to not miss the deal, causing them to hopefully buy it quickly.

The call to action

Customers need to be guided. If you don't tell them what to do next, they may get lost and cause you to lose a potential sale. You need to tell your prospective customers how to order and instill a sense of urgency in them—"call now!"

The call to action gives you certainty that your customers are being guided into taking the action you want them to take, a higher probability that they will act on your offer, and more control over the selling process.

How to order

Make sure you offer as many methods of payment as possible. If your employer is not familiar with newer methods of payment (Square, Dwolla, PayPal, etc.), show her! Allow customers to pay you in as many ways as possible: credit cards, multiple credit cards, multiple payments, business or personal checks, etc.

Give them the option to order by phone, fax, email, or in person. The more options you provide, the easier it will be for someone to give you their money. People don't ask, they assume. If they don't see any other payment options, they assume that you don't accept any other form of payment and move on. If any particular payment method requires multiple steps, explain those steps briefly. Guide the customer. Being flexible when it comes to accepting many methods of payment gives you a better chance to make a sale and creates a wider net for customers who need to have various options to pay.

Your contact information

Displaying your contact information prominently within the sales letter tells your readers that you are a business with a physical location and that you have people available to answer telephone calls, emails, or letters. Depending on your arrangement with your employer, the company's agents can receive incoming calls from your customers. If you need to set up office space, you can rent a virtual office. These are office addresses that companies sell. They allow you to receive mail and incoming calls that can then be transferred to your cellphone or any other telephone you designate.

This puts your readers into a relaxed state of mind in terms of trust. Including your contact information gives you the appearance of a real business and the means for your audience to order from you with ease and be able to talk to a live human being if necessary.

In sum, you can apply the information provided within a sales letter not only to direct marketing, but to many other settings where your employer's offerings may have an audience. For instance, there's a

DVD and music store located in the Times Square subway station in New York City. This store is situated just before you go up the stairs to board the train. It has many television screens displaying action movies, boxing matches, karate, etc., all of which are from DVDs they sell inside the store. Thousands of people pass every day and many stop to watch the television screens. If the owners of this particular store followed these direct marketing concepts, they could add a banner to the videos, displaying a call to action. "Come into the store in the next two minutes and pick up this DVD for only $9.99, a discount of 50%! You have two minutes! See you inside!" If they added a risk reversal line as well, I bet their revenue would grow.

If you're going to sell using direct mail (and I think you should), make sure that you have some level of control over the sales process. You need to understand what is selling and what is not selling. If your employer wants to keep complete control of the data, then you must attempt to find other ways to keep yourself updated as to who on your list is buying from your employer.

NETWORKING AND SOCIAL MEDIA

When it comes to social media, you don't have to spend a lot of money—quite possibly you can spend no money at all. All you need to do is find the connections that will lead to customers (individuals and companies) who make purchases of products and services similar to the ones sold by your employer.

You can find these customers in your own city and country, or in other regions of the world. If you have the right product or service, customers will respond positively because you will be providing solutions to their problems. Today it is exceptionally easy to contact anyone from any company in the world. You need a compelling reason for initial contact, but thanks to social media, everyone is accessible.

The best approach for an employeepreneur is direct contact or marketing with potential customers. This means not only direct mail, but also traditional face-to-face networking or the use of technology to chat or video conference. Technology allows us to extend ourselves beyond the physical limitations of location.

People use social media websites like Facebook, LinkedIn, and Twitter to stay in contact with friends and family and share pictures, stories, information, and more. These websites allow people to reconnect with long-lost friends, make new ones, and stay updated on anything and everything.

Social media marketing is used by many businesses today to gain attention from prospective customers. This works best when the voice of the business disappears and is replaced with the voices of people talking to people. You can be successful because you aren't just a business, you're also a person. Be authentic and use your own voice when communicating through social media channels—you don't want to sound like a faceless corporation. Even LinkedIn, which markets itself as a professional network, looks down on people who join the network with the sole intent to sell.

Content is king when it comes to social media marketing. People are online to learn and share things that make their lives easier and more enjoyable. However, they want to learn these things from other people with similar experiences, not from marketers. They want to learn them from friends and even strangers—as long as they believe the person has nothing directly to gain from sharing the information with them. Users of social media websites don't pay attention to sales pitches directly from businesses—they pay attention to their friends.

When it comes to marketing using social media, your employeepreneur venture needs to act like a regular person who is not pushing people to buy anything. Don't pitch. Be part of the conversation. Add relevant content, help the community find solutions, and then—when they realize how cool you are for not trying to sell—you can secretly sell, sell, sell! People will start to notice your business offerings and start responding to them by buying from you.

If you want to get new customers using social media marketing, then you need to understand that this medium is about connecting with people first. Get to know their needs and wants and only then present your services and products. Sales and profits come after, not before.

I would like to give you some ideas on how to market using some of the most popular social media websites.

Facebook
www.facebook.com

Most of the people on Facebook are looking for news and gossip about their friends. However, they are also consumers. Businesses from all industries are flocking to Facebook, trying to entice consumers to become interested in their products and services. Facebook offers a huge marketing opportunity. But understand that, most likely, you will be looking at the retail side of your employeepreneur venture, and that side is not lucrative unless you sell high-value products and services for your employer.

LinkedIn
www.linkedin.com

LinkedIn is a business networking website for professionals, business owners, and entrepreneurs. This is different from Facebook because even though there are many business professionals on Facebook, business audiences are not at the core of the service. LinkedIn has two levels of membership, free and paid. The free version offers only limited services; the premium service offers unlimited access to everyone on the network.

The LinkedIn premium service is great for networking with other business owners and professionals and establishing your leadership and presence on a local, national, and global scale.

Groups are easy to create on LinkedIn and can be very useful in creating a following for your personal brand and your employer's products and services. You can use groups to sell your services and products directly to your subscribers. This is a key point that distinguishes LinkedIn from Facebook—on LinkedIn, people are absolutely looking for an edge to become more successful within their particular business or industry. If you offer them that edge, you will not only get their business, but you'll become part of their network and your employeepreneur venture will grow exponentially.

Twitter
www.twitter.com

Twitter is a micro-blogging website that allows you to create messages no longer than 140 characters (also known as "tweets"). Twitter is very easy to use. Just visit the website, fill out the signup form, and create an account. All you need is your full name, a twitter handle, a password, and your email address. Choose a handle that identifies what you do. The handle should be cool and catchy, so that prospective customers know immediately what you do and want to follow you. Make sure to use a picture.

After you create your account, you can start following people. That means that every time they "tweet" a message, you'll be able to see it right away. The people who follow you will be able to see your tweets as soon as you post them. This social media platform is amazingly powerful in spreading information across states, countries, and continents in a matter of seconds. On Twitter, if you want people to follow you, you have to follow others. The best way to accomplish this is by creating or sharing interesting content.

To market effectively on Twitter, you need to start following your prospective customers. Twitter provides up-to-date information about what's going on in people's (and companies') minds across the world. You can follow organizations, celebrities, friends, and any other person or entity you find interesting.

Start following everyone who's related to your industry and tune in to what they're saying. This is the best way to find out not only what your employer would be interested in, but also what your industry is craving.

Chapter 17
Customers and Lead Generation

I mentioned before that your employer or boss is actively marketing his services to potential customers in the community, city, or country where he operates and that it would be wise to stay away from retail. As you already know, retail is the sale of goods in small quantities directly to consumers. A business can be a retail or wholesale supplier. A shoe store can sell one or a few pairs of shoes to individual customers (retail), or a fruit company can sell large quantities of fruit at lower cost (wholesale). You may want to stay away from retail when it comes to your employeepreneur venture, because it can create conflicts of interest with your employer or boss.

If you must engage in retail, then you should use a code that would identify your customers in order to distinguish them from your employer's. I truly believe that you should go for big companies or accounts (wholesale). Continuing with the shoe example, you could bring a big account or buyer from another region or part of the world—perhaps someone who wants to place large orders for orphaned children in poor countries in Africa, Asia, or Latin America, or perhaps large orders from a fancy company for their fancy customers.

These kinds of accounts will not only bring you more financial benefits, but they will also save you time. One big account can represent a hundred or a thousand pairs of shoes. And to get that many sales at once, from one customer, saves you from having to find one hundred or one thousand customers.

Depending on what you sell, initiating contact and getting these big customers is not impossible. We already talked about LinkedIn, Twitter, and Facebook as sources where you can find and connect with millions of people and companies all over the world. However, there are many other ways to find and connect with companies in many industries that buy goods (food, toys, equipment, office supplies, etc.) and services (transportation, beauty and wellness, security, etc.). Besides using the Internet to get new customers, you can try the ways described below.

1. Strategic alliance

Regardless of what your employer sells, someone out there has hundreds of customers who buy those products and services. The beauty of creating strategic alliances or partnerships is that you can access hundreds of customers at the same time by going to only one person. Find these strategic people and make them an offer they can't refuse.

2. Referrals

If your customers are satisfied with the products and services your employer provides, then ask them for referrals. This is the easiest and cheapest way to get new customers.

Bringing in these big accounts will increase your salary, give you instant clout, and put you in line for promotions.

Your boss or employer will see the immense value you bring to the company, and making money with your mind will become such an exciting hobby that even when you go on vacation you will be connecting with people and sourcing for business. If you can afford it, go to expensive resorts and hotels. Depending on what your employer sells, you can find rich and influential people in these places. Think of your vacation as an investment.

There's no logical reason not to go after big accounts. The same presentation skills you used to present to your boss or employer can be used to present to your potential customers. Remember to find out everything you can about their needs and wants before you approach each customer. They should feel that you know their most pressing problems and pains and that you've already created a customized or tailored solution for their specific needs.

What if you don't sell any physical goods, and your employer only offers services? If you work in the service industry and the people have to come to your employer's business in order to receive their service, as with a hotel, then you can use the same concept to attract big customers who need service. Hotels love groups. They are the equivalent of wholesale in other kinds of businesses. They know that they can't get every single group that is out there. Your help would be invaluable.

Depending on your arrangement with your employer, all you would need to do is put the group

head in contact with a sales manager in your hotel—
and then, magic!

It doesn't matter if you sell products or services. If
there's a customer who wants or needs your offerings,
you can create the connection and bring them in as
customers. It's that simple.

Keep in mind that you are not a company. You
are nimble and free—no inventory, no overhead, no
employees, and no headaches. You are an employeepreneur, and like a honeybee, you make things grow
by touching them with your intellect. You create
your own strategies when it comes to getting customers. In addition, you don't have to make the mistakes of traditional companies. For instance, when
some companies are selling or presenting their
offers to customers, they use a "buy now" approach.
You want to stay away from this approach. When
these companies present their offers, they expect
customers to be ready to buy right now. If the customer is not ready, they move on. These companies
don't realize that a customer may want what they
offer but may not be ready to buy at the time of the
advertising.

She may instead be ready in the near future. She
may be interested now but may not have the money,
or she may have some interest now but need to think
about it. It is always good to give the customer opportunities to stay in touch with you (via telephone, email,
text message, or social media) in case they want to
buy later or ask questions about your offering. This
approach will not only help you sell, it will also help
you create a bank of leads.

This can be your competitive advantage in two ways: (1) by creating a relationship with your customers, you secure them as customers forever, and (2) by creating a bank of leads, you ensure that you can have a group of customers who need or want to buy your employer's products and services on a regular basis.

The foundation of any relationship is trust. Make sure that you build on that foundation by honoring your promises and delivering quality products and services.

Your bank of leads will prove to be invaluable whenever you need a salary increase, because your leads represent potential buyers of your employer's products or services. This gives you the opportunity to raise your salary as often as you want because you know that they are interested in buying what you sell.

Imagine that your employer has inventory that he or she doesn't know what to do with. You can sell it to your list. Or imagine your employer has a slow season in the service area of the business. You can sell those services to your bank of leads at a discount or full price. The sky is the limit when it comes to the possibilities you can find in your particular industry and company, if you look for them.

So how do you create a big bank of leads? The first and most important thing to keep in mind is that every time you present your offerings you should be looking for one of two things: a sale or a lead. Today, most people want to create relationships with their service providers. Many tactics that used to work in the past don't work anymore, like cold calling or selling door to door. Customers today are developing relationships with their vendors and this doesn't leave a lot of room for peddlers.

Make sure that your sales and marketing approach is aligned to present not only "buy now" offers but also that it gives potential customers the opportunity to connect with you. Consider leads to be the lifeblood of your employeepreneur venture. Generating leads is about making connections. Remember that people know other people and that you should never underestimate any potential lead that comes your way. The smallest person can connect you with the biggest person. Always keep this in mind as you continue on your journey of discovery.

You should have a system in place to work your leads in an effective way. When dealing with leads, you should be familiar with these three aspects: (1) getting the lead, (2) managing the lead, and (3) converting the lead into a sale.

GETTING LEADS

The business world was set up with a hunter's mentality. Hunters hunt every day and try to find their daily bread by approaching customers and asking them to buy now. There's nothing wrong with hunting, but when that's all you do, then you have to hunt forever. The best way to create a bank of leads is by farming.

Farmers always have food because they farm seeds, animals, and other resources. They don't have to go out in the cold winter to look for food. The best way to farm for leads, regardless of the industry you're in, is by inserting lead capture forms into every single one of your advertising and marketing efforts.

To get the contact information of those who are not ready to buy now, you can do various things. You can, for example, direct them to watch a video or download a report to get more information about what your employer offers. To see the video or download the report, you can ask them to submit their email address or telephone number. If the report has important information that they can't get anywhere else, you can ask them for their office or home postal address to mail a hard copy directly to them.

If they give you their home address, that means you have their permission to market to them in their home. You could also ask them to call a telephone number to listen to special information about your offerings—in which case, you capture their phone number. Any of these methods would give you a lead that you can then use to start creating a relationship with a person who is obviously interested in what you offer.

Remember that your employer already has most of the resources you will need in place. If for example you need to build a landing page, your webmaster can help you. It's simple and inexpensive to create a landing page. You would also be able to place videos for your leads to watch and they can also download reports or any other type of document. Your webmaster could also help you to set up mailing campaigns and the back-office technological stuff that go along with them.

MANAGING LEADS

Managing leads is just as important as getting them. If your prospective customer has agreed to stay in contact with you through email, telephone, or postal mail, you now can communicate with this person and keep her informed about the products and services she showed interest in. Remember that this person represents future income or salary and that if you don't keep talking to her, when she's ready to buy, she will not remember you, and will find a different provider.

Don't forget that she has a lot of options. It's your decision how often you want to communicate. If you have her email address, telephone number, or postal address, it means that you have permission to send her marketing material. If you have her email address, you could email her once a week.

If you have your potential customer's postal address, mailing once a month would be cost effective and appropriate. A postcard would do. Postcards are cheap and very effective to stay in touch with quick reminders or just to say hello. All you need to do is to remind your prospect that you are there if she needs you, and why you are the best option around.

CONVERTING LEADS

Converting the lead means that the prospect goes from being an interested prospective customer to actually buying what you are selling. When this happens, this person needs to be moved to another list. In the beginning, you can manage your bank of leads on your computer or in a notebook, but as you get more and more leads and customers, you might need to consider the services of contact management software. A simple search on the Internet will provide many options in this space. Watch their demo videos and choose the one you feel most comfortable with when the right time comes.

As soon as someone changes his status from lead to customer, this person is under your care and protection beyond the predictable "hello I am here" communication. You must treat her like a queen, so that she brings many more customers to your employer. The customer has complete control of the conversion. Your job is to stay present, and to keep your message in front of your prospect at all times until they decide to buy. Can you do that? It shouldn't be that hard.

Chapter 18
Legal Issues and Negotiations

Depending on your relationship with your employer, you should already know what you can expect in terms of honesty and integrity. However, it is always a good idea to protect yourself as much as possible.

Most likely, your employer will be using a fancy lawyer to structure any deal with you. One thing you can do to make sure you are protected and that you will not lose your money as an employeepreneur is to have a lawyer of your own review the contracts or agreements to make sure that there's nothing improper.

If your lawyer gives you the green light, you can proceed. If you trust your employer, you don't even have to mention that you are using a lawyer. It all depends on the kind of deal you are working on and presenting: be flexible and don't scare your employer. If you get an idea for software that could change the industry or a multimillion-dollar client or deal, get a lawyer from the start. If your lawyer reviews the agreement, you should be protected. Mentioning the involvement of a lawyer might scare your employer away from doing business with you.

Remember, if your employer decides to enter a partnership arrangement with you, in her eyes she is doing you a huge favor. She's giving you the opportunity to make money far beyond your limited weekly salary. In her eyes, you should be grateful. Give her every indication that you trust her—but still be sure to protect yourself just in case.

Deals can be structured in a wide variety of ways. Be flexible. Don't push. You need to allow your employer to take the bigger cut from your initial ventures. The time will come when your negotiating powers will grow, but in the beginning, understand that you have little leverage. This is a big opportunity you are being given. You are being allowed to run your own company inside of your boss's business without overhead or headaches.

These types of employer/employee joint ventures are rare and delicate. Your employer will keep an eye out for any signs of trouble to provide an excuse to pull the plug on your employeepreneur venture. Don't allow that to happen. Be humble. Above all, make your employer feel that she can trust you 100%.

There are some things you need to be absolutely clear about before you sign any contract or agreement.

COMPENSATION

Compensation has many faces. Some people want stocks, others want upfront fees or commissions, while others just want paid time off. What do you want? Think about it. You deserve to be well compensated. Don't be intimidated by the fact that you are also an employee at your working place. Don't be greedy, but let your boss know that you expect to be fairly compensated for the additional revenue you will be providing the business.

RESIDUAL INCOME

Let me give you a scenario to explain residual income in a way that sinks deep into your mind. Let's suppose that you bring a big client to your employer. Everything is going great with your job and your employeepreneur venture is standing on solid ground. But all of a sudden you get news that, for personal reasons, you need to relocate and your company doesn't have a branch in the city you have to move to.

If you stipulated in the contract that you are to receive compensation from all transactions your customers conduct with your employer, even if you are no longer with the company, you will get paid a fee every month from all the customers you brought to your employer. However, it doesn't matter how nice and sweet your employer may be, if this is not stipulated in the contract or if it's only word of mouth, rest assured that somewhere along the way, it will feel "awkward" to pay a fee when you are no longer with the company. Remember, corporations are not people, even though people run them; they don't feel remorse or empathy.

Most likely, the customers you bring could continue doing business with your employer for as long as you stay with the company or long after you're gone. Make sure that you specify clearly on the contract that you are entitled to residual income for the business life of all your customers with your employer.

SURVIVAL BENEFICIARY

We all have an expiration date. Make sure that you have written into the contract the person or persons you want to continue receiving the benefits of your work in case you unexpectedly pass away.

Depending on how hard you work, you could end up with deals making millions of dollars—you don't want your employer keeping all that money when it could be helping your family. Make sure that the agreement you sign stipulates this clearly. If your employer refuses to do this, consult with your lawyer to find ways to make sure that your money finds its way to your family and not your employer's bank account.

NEW PRODUCTS, SERVICES, AND INNOVATIONS

The same principle applies here. If you create new products or services for your employer, to whom do those products and services belong? Make sure to stipulate clauses in the contract at the beginning to avoid painful situations later on.

In conversation, everything can seem perfect, but when money starts showing up (and believe me, if you apply the strategies in this book, money will show up), agreements fail, loyalties change, friendships and relationships crack, and employee/employer relationships turn sour.

You can avoid conflicts by making everything crystal clear from the beginning. This conversation may not be pleasant, but if you employer doesn't want to agree with the clauses protecting you (and herself) in the contract from the beginning, be careful with any deals you make based on word of mouth or handshake.

Keep in mind that, if you are acting as an employeepreneur, you have the control of your intellectual properties. You can give the exclusive rights of your creations to your employer (or not!), lease them, or offer them to your whole industry. It's all up to you.

Chapter 19
Gratitude

When you arise in the morning, think of what a precious privilege it is to be alive, to breathe, to think, to enjoy, and to love.
⁓Marcus Aurelius

Everything you have ever owned has come to you from the hands of others. As a baby, you received love, attention, and guidance from your parents, family members, and family friends. Today as an employee, you receive benefits created by your employer. This allows you to have all of the material things you currently own: your car, your house, your clothes, etc. However, many people often forget to be grateful for all of the things that they have. The German theologian Meister Eckhart said, "If the only prayer you said in your life was 'thank you,' that would be enough." A lot of people say thank you by default, like when someone does something nice for them—when a stranger holds the door, for example. But what is a *thank you* prayer? What does that even mean? The dictionary defines the word gratitude as "a feeling of thankfulness, acknowledgement, and appreciation."

Jesus said that we should be "thankful for the things we have and also give thanks for the things we wish to have, as if we already have them." If you believe in a superior being, whatever name you attribute to it, give thanks for everything you have.

Why say "thank you" for our current and future possessions? Because by doing so, we stay connected to the things we have, so that we can be aware of them and enjoy them, while we go after the things we want to have. Not being grateful for what we already possess is one of the main causes of suffering in our society.

None of the possessions in the world can make you happy if you don't have motivations that go beyond those material possessions. A house itself is not happiness. Happiness is turning that house into a home—with a partner, children, visits from friends and family, harmony, etc. A car itself does not provide happiness. Happiness is where that car can take you (or the pleasurable feeling of driving the car)—to a friend's wedding, a vacation, or a restaurant you love.

Material possessions are purely a means to an end. If you try to make material things responsible for your happiness, you'll only end up miserable and disappointed. Many of the richest people on the planet—past and present—have lived miserable lives because they tried to turn their material possessions into their happiness. It is impossible. We are spiritual beings—all exists for our spiritual enjoyment.

Make it a habit to say "thank you" throughout each day and always be thankful for everything you already have.

How can this simple act of giving thanks be so powerful? Here are a few reasons why.

Saying "thank you" will remind you of all the good things you have in your life. It will make you think about your family and friends and other loved ones, as well as everything you own.

Saying "thank you" will remind you how lucky you are to be alive, to be able to see each new day, and be able to enjoy it with the people you love.

Saying "thank you" will remind you to appreciate the people in your life, because when you acknowledge and thank them for everything they mean to you and do for you, your relationships will grow stronger.

Saying "thank you" will remind you that even the negative things that come into your life have a purpose. Try not to get stressed when things don't go according to your plan. A negative situation means that something needs your attention. You need to stop, pay attention, fix it, learn the lesson in it, and continue growing.

Saying "thank you" for what you have will constantly remind you to enjoy everything in your life and this joy, in turn, will attract all the new things you want.

Let's face it, we'll never have absolutely everything we want. I don't mean that we should just accept our share in life and be done with it. What I mean is that getting to a point where we want nothing else is impossible, because our nature is to want more—more things, more experiences, and more knowledge. There's always something new to experience, learn, fix, sell, or buy. It's part of everyday life. It's human nature to grow by experiencing new things every day.

Chapter 20
Goal Setting

A man, as a general rule, owes very little to what he is born with—a man is what he makes of himself.
~ Alexander Graham Bell

The number one reason most people don't make their dreams come true is because they don't set goals. Goal setting is similar to sending a message of what you want out into society, or to the universe, if you prefer. A goal is a proclamation to the world of your intentions. Even though you organize your goals in private, they soon become public through the power of your intentions and attention. Making goal declarations is the best way to engrave your desires onto the fabric of your subconscious mind, which communicates directly with the universal mind or all the minds on the planet. The universe or the fabric of life (if you prefer) then bends over backwards to give you what you want. All that is necessary is that you step out of the way and let it do its work.

Setting goals ensures that our dreams and desires stay fresh in our conscious and subconscious minds. I am sure you've seen or heard about *The Secret*, the movie that initiated a global movement about the power of the mind to attract what we want.

The concept is true, but the producers and actors omitted two fundamental factors in realizing one's dreams: 1) self-esteem (which we covered in chapter one), and 2) goal setting.

Without these two elements *The Secret* remains a secret.

In my personal opinion, it's not so much about getting the object of your dreams and desires; you will get that, no doubt. But it's also about the way you will feel when you know that you're working with all your resources towards the attainment of your goal.

Everything that comes into your field of awareness will be useful in some way to get you closer to your goals. Your job will become the main focus because, regardless of what you do for a living, you will have ample resources there to begin your journey.

But awareness and good feelings alone won't do the trick. You also need discipline and persistence. The combination of these four factors (self-esteem, goal setting, thinking constantly about your dreams, and working on discovering new opportunities and increasing your commercial value at work) will give you the financial results you seek in terms of pay raises, promotions, and recognition.

One of the best authors in terms of goal setting I know is Brian Tracy. His book *Goals!* is one the best books on goal setting on the market today.

Brian Tracy offers a very interesting way of setting goals. He writes his goals in present tense, as if they were already a reality. For example, he doesn't say, "I will quit smoking." Instead he says, "I am a non-smoker." Brian advises that when you set your goals, you should always use *I* followed by an action verb. For example, "I drive the car of my dreams in six months," or "I earn x amount of money by the end of eight months."

Another exercise is to write 10 goals on a blank piece of paper. Once you have all 10 goals on the paper, ask yourself this question: "If I could wave a magic wand and achieve any goal on this list within twenty-four hours, which one goal would have the greatest positive impact on my life?" Put a circle around your chosen goal and then transfer it to the top of a clean sheet of paper.

1. Write it down clearly.

2. Set a deadline for achieving this goal.

3. Identify the obstacles you'll need to overcome to achieve this goal.

4. Identify the knowledge and skills you will need to achieve it.

5. Set priorities on the steps you'll implement to reach this goal.

The most important thing is becoming aware of your dreams and desires. Talk about them, read them every day, and believe that you deserve every single one of them.

If you take these steps, the information you have covered in this book will be of greater benefit to you. It will have greater value to you and you will realize your financial dreams.

Chapter 21
Creating Your Desired Lifestyle

Your job is a stepping-stone to the life you want to live. You probably started working in your present job because it offered what you were looking for, or perhaps just because it was all that was available.

By now you may have realized that in these economic times, it would be hard to reach your goals on a fixed salary and inflation-adjusted raises. It just doesn't add up. The purpose of this book has been to show you that having the life you want while having a job is indeed possible. The only remaining thing to figure out is what your dream life will look like. What do you really want out of life and out of your employeepreneur venture?

The following questions have helped me clarify my goals and dreams. Take time to answer them and revisit them often. They will keep you on the right path.

How do you want to design your new lifestyle?

What are your relationships like with your partner, children, friends, extended family members, etc.? How do you want those relationships to change, if at all?

Where do you want to live? What kind of house do you want? What does it look like? What is the style and color and how many rooms does it have? Does it have a swimming pool?

What is your dream work schedule? How many hours do you want to work and how many days a week? How much money do you want to make every year? What will constitute success for you in your new lifestyle? Who will you work with and who will be your customers? What kind of relationship will you have with your customers?

What is your idea of the perfect vacation? Where will you go and what will you do? What countries do you dream of visiting? What activities will you enjoy the most?

What do you consider to be important in your life now? How do you think that could change when you start living your desired lifestyle?

Will you either start to exercise or exercise more, to become healthier and to live longer? Will you pamper yourself and practice techniques to lead a balanced life, like doing yoga and eating a healthy diet?

How will you spend your time off? What will you do? Where will you go? What will make you happy every day? What will be your number one reason for getting out of bed?

With whom will you want to spend your new life?

When we have big dreams, sometimes we aren't clear about how much things cost or how we can break it down into smaller parts. For example, how much money do we need on a daily or monthly basis to accomplish our goals and maintain our dream lifestyle?

Everything may seem complicated and too difficult to achieve if you look only at the big picture. But once we achieve clarity on the individual parts, we can determine exactly what we need to do.

In the chart on the next page, you can see how easy it is to describe and financially simplify the amount of money you need, on a monthly and daily basis, to live the life you want.

In the first column, list the things you want. In the second, list how much they cost per month. In the third, list how much they cost per day. In the fourth, write down the reasons why you want these things.

Try it and you will see how this exercise can bring you clarity regarding the things you need in order to start living the life you're dreaming of.

Item	Monthly Cost	Daily Cost	Why?
	$	$	

Once this exercise is complete, you'll have a clear

and firm understanding of your finances and the size of the projects or customers you need to bring to your employer. Depending on the lifestyle you want for yourself, the amount of money that you need to earn will vary. You have to be creative and flexible with your employer's resources. Use them—they are available to you.

This clarity of purpose will supercharge you with an energy you've never experienced before. Your attitude will change completely and your inspiration and zest for life will flow from you like an electrical charge going haywire.

Afterword

The benefits you will bring to your employer's business once you become an employeepreneur will set you apart from all of your co-workers and put you in line for quick promotions to higher positions if you want them.

You can help your employer realize that businesses all over the world lost their way with the advent of the Industrial Revolution. Many companies today still behave with the same limiting mindsets of 50 or even 100 years ago. They ignore employees' knowledge and insight, even when these employees know more than management about the customers. Management creates a business plan and retreats from the battlefield, leaving employees to handle customers every hour of the day.

Your employer doesn't know what you can do. For him, you represent a job description—a pair of hands with a set of tasks to execute day in and day out.

He doesn't understand that you can make his business prosperous beyond his wildest dreams. Maybe you didn't know it either, but now you do. This book has shown it to you, and it has also shown you how easy it can be.

You deserve to live the life you dream about. If, financially speaking, you are not living it right now, it is because you are not making the amount of money you need. Help your boss make more money and you will start living your fantasy life.

Take action today!